The cookbook for easy, family-friendly, flavor-packed meals you can make any day of the week

ground beef
RECIPES

Jan Charles

Ground Beef Recipes

The cookbook for easy, family friendly, flavor packed meals you can make any day of the week.

Jan Charles

Design (cover and illustrations): Ashraful Alam, www.aswmness.net.

eBook edition formatted by Writing Nights in 2016. (www.writingnights.org)

As with everything in my life, this book is lovingly dedicated to my Horde of precious darlings:

Brent, Ricky, Chase, Lanthe, Bladen, Boone, Kinsley and Joey

Who taste tested every recipe in this book

And in loving memory of my Dads

Tommy Charles

Who taught me to love food

And

Joe Hickerson

Who taught me to love teaching

Table of

Contents

Table of Contents... 5

Preface 13

Grounded in History – The History of
Ground Beef.. 14

What's the Beef? 15

Spice in Your Life 18

Fat Trick 20

Choice and Use... 21

Health and Safety 23

Au Naturel... 24

The Recipes 26

Hamburgers... 27

All American Cheeseburger 31

Cottage Pie 32

Shepherd's Pie with Potato Crust 36

Cabbage Rolls 38

Sloppy Joes 41

Easy Cheesy Tacos 43

Beef Breakfast Sausages 45

Salisbury Steak 47

Greek Baked Ziti 49

Hamburgers Diane 51

Dirty rice 53

One Pot Spaghetti and Meat Sauce 56

Homestyle Meatloaf 58

Beef and Macaroni 60

Beef and Cheese Manicotti 62

Mexican Lasagna 64

Southwestern Meatloaf 66

Swiss Burgers in Tomato Gravy 68

Beef and Tomato with Polenta Crust 70

Jamaican Beef Patties 72

Simple, Perfect Chili 75

Ground Beef Recipes

Chili Topped Potatoes.............................. 77

Walking Tacos.. 79

Chili Bowls – Petro's... 80

Smothered Enchiladas............................. 81

Spaghetti with Meat Sauce....................... 83

Beef and Cheese Ravioli Bake.................. 85

Hamburger Steak with Mushroom Onion Gravy 87

Perfect Party Meatballs 89

Cocktail Meatballs 91

Greek Burgers with Tzatziki Sauce......... 93

Bierocks (German Meat Turnovers)........ 95

Meatballs Stroganoff 97

Spaghetti Pie 99

Old-Fashioned Meatloaf 101

Mini Pepper Relish Meatloaves............. 103

Tex-Mex Meatballs in Red Chile Sauce 105

Three Cheese Beef Pasta Shells.............. 107

World's Best Lasagna 109

Railroad Pie... 112

Mince and Tatties 114

Spaghetti Bolognese 117

Asian Ground Beef, Pepper and Onion Sauté 119

Korean Beef Rice Bowls.......................... 121

Asian Beef and Cabbage Salad 123

Mediterranean Beef Pitas 124

Korean Ground Beef Egg Rolls.............. 125

Ground Beef Bulgogi.............................. 127

Asian Inspired Ground Beef.................. 128

Sesame Garlic Beef Tacos....................... 129

Quick Pickled Cucumbers and Cabbage
.... 131

Eastern European Kotlety 132

Serbian Ground Beef, Veggie, and Potato Bake... 133

Asian Lettuce Wraps 135

Simple Taco Soup 136

Poor Man's Beef Wellington 137

Mexican Pizza 139

Meatball Sub Hot Pockets...................... 141

Hobo Beans 143

Ground Beef Recipes

Cheeseburger Casserole 144

Slow Cooker Beef and Cheese Pasta 146

Super Nachos 148

Porcupine Meatballs 150

Tennessee Meatloaf 151

Easy Blue Ribbon Chili 153

Italian Ground Beef Casserole with Biscuit Topping 154

Double Stuffed Taco Potatoes 156

Stuffed Spaghetti Squash with Tomato and Ground Beef 158

Cabbage and Ground Beef Soup 160

Ground Beef Noodle Soup Recipe 162

Easy Stuffed Zucchini 163

Real Deal Hamburger Helper 165

Picadillo Cubano 166

Swedish Meatballs 168

Cheeseburger Gnocchi 170

One Pot Cheeseburger Casserole 172

Italian Wedding Soup 174

Stuffed French Bread Sandwiches 176

5-Ingredient Chili 178

Cheeseburger Egg Rolls 179

Enchilada Zucchini Boats....................... 181

Tamale Pie 183

Beef and Barley Soup 185

Cheeseburger Soup 186

Hashweh, Ground Beef and Rice with
Nuts 187

Kofta Kebabs with Tzatziki.................... 189

Stuffed Eggplant 192

Kheema, Indian Ground Beef with Peas194

Spicy Indian Style Meatballs 196

Moussaka 197

Greek Bifteki 200

Greek Souzoukaklia 201

Pastitsio 202

Keftedes (Greek Meatballs).................... 204

Greek Lasagna 205

Yemistes – Greek Style Stuffed Tomatoes
.... 207

Youverlakia - Greek Meatball Soup with Egg Lemon Sauce 209

Sauces and Seasonings 211

Ricky's Salsa 212

Italian Seasoning 213

Chili Powder 214

Greek Seasoning Blend 215

Taco Seasoning 216

Curry Powder 217

Chipotle Salsa 218

Montreal Steak Seasoning 220

Cajun Spice Mix 221

Homemade Marinara Sauce Recipe 222

Enchilada Sauce 223

Stocks and Pastries 224

Corn Muffin Mix 225

Homemade Ranch Dressing Seasoning Mix 226

Homemade Italian Breadcrumbs 227

Pie Crust 228

Celery Salt 229

Rotel Copycat Recipe 230

Chicken Broth 231

Beef Stock 232

Condensed Cream of Mushroom Soup
Substitute... 234

Garam Masala 235

Fines Herbs... 236

About the Author 237

GROUNDED IN HISTORY - THE HISTORY OF GROUND BEEF

Ground beef, which is also sometimes called mince or beef mince in the United Kingdom and other places outside the United States, is simply beef that has been chopped or minced into very small pieces. It's used in all kinds of recipes, from the classic American hamburger, to casseroles and wraps. It's incredibly versatile, and is great to pair with flavors from all over the world.

Chopped, ground or minced beef is not new. There were pies made with savory meat fillings in ancient Rome. Steak tartare, made with very finely chopped, highly seasoned steak goes back to medieval Russia. Germans pounded beef until very tender, in order to produce the original Hamburg steak. In America, Delmonico's in New York introduced a hamburger under the name of Hamburg steak in 1834. Charles and Frank Menches placed the hamburger on a bun in 1885 at the Erie County Fair.

At the end of the Civil War, in one of America's first health food movements, Dr. James Henry Salisbury developed the dish which came to be known as Salisbury steak, as a means of treating Civil War soldiers who suffered constitutional issues following their service. Dr. Salisbury prescribed the patties made with wholesome beef, seasoned and broiled to be taken three times a day.

The hamburger on a bun was fully entrenched in America as early as 1912, and the first hamburger stand opened as White Castle in Wichita, Kansas in 1921. By 1938 the cheeseburger was a growing fad, and the term burger began to refer to a range of sandwiches made with ground meats or seafood. In the years since, ground meats have been made into countless dishes by cooks around the world.

Americans normally refer to the terms ground beef and hamburger interchangeably. In other parts of the world mince is more common, as mince pies were originally made with ground, minced and spiced meats.

WHAT'S THE BEEF?

In the US, ground beef can contain a maximum of 30% fat. In Europe the maximum amount of fat allowed in generally much lower, about 15% in most countries. Labeling in the United States requires that ground beef is labeled with the fat content. You'll see this listed as 70/30, 85/15, 90/20, etc. The first number indicates the amount of lean meat, and the second number is the percentage of fat in that particular mixture.

In the US we've been convinced that fat is bad, and as a result, we often automatically look for the least amount of fat in a product. However, not only have recent studies been showing that fat is not only not horrible, it's also necessary. Health concerns aside, when talking about ground beef it's important to remember that fat equals flavor. Without some fat in the mix, your ground beef recipe is going to probably be very dry and with far less flavor than if it had a bit of fat left in. The amount of fat is up to you however, and if fat is really a concern, there are ways to remove almost all of it – I'll tell you how in a bit. Just be sure if you remove the fat, you make up for it with herbs, spices and the correct level of salt and pepper.

Because nutrition research is exploding, and we're learning more and more every day, I encourage you to dig into some of the recent studies about natural fats and the nutrition they contain. By the time you read this, I'm sure the research will have revealed even more, so I'm not going to go into all of it. But I will say that the fats of organic, grass fed or pasture raised animals that seem to be actually beneficial, so do your research and make your decisions based on good science.

Beef is actually very high in protein of course. But in my own opinion, the more important thing about beef is that it leads to a very high degree of satiety. You feel more full with less food. That's win-win right there. And it's certainly easy to get picky eaters to eat a variety of recipes with ground beef, so it's a great way to expand the repertoire of the pickiest diners.

When buying ground beef, you want a nice, rich red color, and the fat should be marbled throughout the package. Keep in mind that the more fat in the product, the less red it will be; the higher fat content will make the beef more pink. I tend to buy ground chuck. It comes from muscle that is used, which means more flavor, but is also relatively lean. If you want super lean, but less flavor, go for ground sirloin.

If you are really concerned about safety, or about the fat content or your food, then you can certainly grind your own if you want. You don't even have to have a meat grinder – it can be done in a food processor. Whichever equipment you use, make sure to cut the beef into small cubes – about 1 inch each, and then chill them well. Once cold, place the beef in small batches (about 1/3 pound each batch) in the bowl of a food processor (or just run it through your grinder), and process the beef cubes in pulses. Make sure you include about 10% fat, otherwise you'll have a very lean, but very dry, less flavorful result. Make sure you pulse – if you work in short bursts of about 1 second each, you'll have much better results. If you allow the processor to run continuously, you'll end up with a thick mush from the heat of the friction of the blades.

If you'll be using herbs, spices or other ingredients, you can go ahead and toss them into the <u>food processor</u> with the beef cubes – flavoring will be really well incorporated into the mixture as you process the beef. If you want to make burgers, use a coarser grind, and season with kosher salt and good black pepper in the processor. If making a meatloaf or meatballs, grind the meat a bit more.

For the most part, I use 90/10 – so I use ground beef that is 90% lean meat, 10% fat. When I brown the beef I then drain off the fat that collects in the skillet. (You can save that fat to cook with by the way, and I do. Nothing goes to waste in my kitchen, and it makes incredible potatoes). I also try to make sure that I'm using organic, grass fed beef. It is more expensive, granted. But you'll see that the majority of my recipes use relatively little beef in ratio to other ingredients. So I've chosen to buy higher quality and use less of it. I like the trade off, but if you have a seriously limited budget, buy what you can afford. I get that entirely – I've certainly been there.

Keep in mind that more fat also means more shrinkage. Leaner ground beef will lose less fat in the cooking process, so will shrink less. The recipes in this book can be swapped for higher fat content beef, no problem. But remember the final result will have less volume. Not that big a deal for many dishes, especially stuffing or casseroles, but it can seriously shrink a burger down to a fraction of the size of the bun, and your meatloaf can almost disappear.

When talking about ground beef, there are several things that can be included if the label just says 'hamburger'. This can't contain more than 30% fat, but often is made up of the all the trimmings the butcher collects when trimming other cuts. So you may have chuck or sirloin or brisket in the mix, which is why hamburger often has such a rich, beefy flavor. The fat content also contributes to the flavor.

Some grinds are more expensive, and if the label says the package contains the grind of a particular cut, then that's all that's allowed to be in the package. The fat content can also be high though – so just because it lists ground round it's not necessarily low in fat. If the package says lean however, it must be lower in fat, less than 22% fat. Extra lean ground beef must be less than 15%. Use this guideline when looking at the fat content of particular cuts/grinds:

Ground chuck: 80-85% lean

Ground round: 85-90% lean

Ground sirloin: 90-92% lean

There are a couple of hints about cooking with ground beef (or any ground meat, and almost every recipe you'll find here can use ground chicken, turkey or pork). The first is to brown it correctly if you'll be using it in tacos, casseroles or stuffing it into something. Use a big skillet – you want a large surface area to work with. Part of what you are doing is heating the food so that the water evaporates – if you squeeze it into a small pan, you'll end up steaming the meat instead of really browning it. So give yourself a large piece of real estate. Also, heat your skillet before you add the beef. That helps keep it from sticking.

Secondly, really work on the beef while it cooks. You don't need to add fat to the pan (unless you have a super lean product), but you do want to really work on the beef to get very small pieces. Just keep working it with a spatula or wooden spoon. The smaller the pieces, the more water will evaporate out, and the more fat will render away. This means more flavor – always a good thing! The browning won't take long – use medium heat, and you'll be done in about 10-15 minutes. You just want a nice, rich brown color and no more pink shows. That's all there is to that.

FAT TRICK

I mentioned before that if fat is really a concern, you can use a trick to get rid of almost all of it. This works best with recipes that have a ton of additional spices added – chili or tacos are great. Once you brown the beef, drain off the fat from the pan and put the browned beef in a colander or small strainer. Then run very hot to boiling water over it – the hot water will take away most of the remaining fat. Keep in mind it also takes away flavor and texture – so maybe try it once and see how you like the result.

Make sure you brown and drain the fat off ground beef before you add vegetables to the skillet. The water from the veggies (onion, peppers, garlic, tomatoes) will steam the beef and make it harder to get the most flavor from the meat. You'll also lose a lot of the flavor from the sautéed veggies if you drain the fat off after the veggies have started cooking. That's no fun.

CHOICE AND USE

If you are going to be using the ground beef in burgers or meatballs or meatloaf, the number one thing to remember is that the more you work with ground meat, the tougher it can become. So you want to mix it only until the flavorings or ingredients are worked in, then stop. A great trick for making sure everything gets well mixed in without over working the meat is to combine all the ingredients you are adding to the meat in a separate bowl, and combine those thoroughly. Then you can work the flavorings or ingredients in without working the meat more than you have to.

Ground beef is great to buy in bulk and stash in the freezer too. Make sure you use a nice heavy plastic wrap or freezer bag, and freeze in ½ or 1 pound packages. I know a lot of folks who brown beef off to jump start meals, and then freeze the ground beef once it's cooked. I don't do it, but only because it seems to involve extra steps and dishes, since browning beef only takes a few minutes. But everyone has their own schedule and set up – so try it and see if it helps you out. I find it easiest to buy in bulk, divide the beef up into recipe portions, and just freeze it raw.

I will give you an easy way to work with frozen beef if you need to brown it and forgot to defrost it. This is horrible culinary technique, but it works, and sometimes that's the most important thing. Put a skillet over medium low heat, add the frozen beef, and cover the skillet. You won't get the evaporation and browning you would from unfrozen, but hopefully you're more organized than I am and won't ever have to do this. After just a few minutes, flip the frozen beef over. The portion in contact with the skillet will have begun to thaw and cook, and you can scrape it off. While you're doing this, the side in contact with the skillet will also begin to thaw. Just keep flipping and scraping. It takes about 20 minutes to brown a pound of frozen beef this way. Like I said – you won't win awards in a cooking competition, but you can feed your ravenously hungry kids much more quickly.

HEALTH AND SAFETY

All right – real quick, let's talk about safety. The main contaminants of ground beef, which can make you seriously ill, are E. coli, salmonella and listeria. Those aren't very nice things to serve to your family, but luckily it's not difficult to maintain standards which ensure the safety of your food.

Primarily, make sure your hands, work surfaces and utensils are super clean. That's the primary way to avoid illness and contamination. Keep meats and vegetables separate during cooking and prep, and use a good quality soap for cleaning everything you use.

Ground beef can be particularly susceptible to bacterial contamination because grinding exposes more surface area to possible contaminants. The cook news is that cooking destroys bacteria, which is why the USDA recommends cooking beef to a minimum temperature of 160F or 72C. The easiest way to check internal temperatures of beef is with a probe thermometer – easy to find at big box stores or online. The downside is that many people prefer a medium or medium rare, and 160 is much higher than the 135 that is medium rare for a steak. However, in this instance we're talking about ground beef, so just use your head as well as your taste buds.

One final thing – a few years back I kept seeing recipes that called for ground beef that had been boiled instead of browned in a pan. Of course, I had to do it myself to see why it was such a thing. Basically, you cover it with water, stir well, bring to a boil and cook until brown through, stirring to keep breaking it up. I have to say, I couldn't figure out the benefit to the process. You do end up with a weak broth, but it has very little body or flavor. I stuck mine in the fridge and removed the fat later, but the broth wasn't flavorful enough to do much with. It probably did contain some protein, and you could use it to cook rice or quinoa if you wish to recapture those nutrients. The boiling would most likely remove more fat than browning, but it's easier just to rinse the browned beef under very hot water if that's what you are looking to do. It took longer to cook as well, since the water had to come up to temperature. But if you need for some reason to boil your ground beef instead of browning it, it's simple to do.

AU NATUREL.

I don't use processed or packaged food anymore. I learned some years back to make my own mixes and seasoning blends. I've included the recipes for the ones in this cookbook – so you'll get about 20 or so recipes to make your own Italian seasoning, taco seasoning, ranch dressing mix and many more. But if you're new to cooking, feel free to use packaged products. The amounts are still the same – 2 cups marinara is the same as a 15-ounce bottle of jarred sauce, and the amounts of taco or ranch dressing mix are the same as 1 package unless another measurement is given. But – give the scratch versions a try. You'll save acres of money, get rid of preservatives and chemicals, and get much more flavor. Once or twice and you'll be a convert. Promise.

The Recipes

HAMBURGERS

I have a serious love affair with the burger. I don't care what it is, I'll eventually try to make a burger out of it. Over the years I've made dozens of burgers using beef, pork, chicken, turkey, shrimp, salmon – and I've mimicked classic dishes such as larb gai, lasagna, Thanksgiving dinner, chili, and topped my burgers with everything from hash browns, cole slaw, fried eggs, mixed greens, sausage patties, heirloom tomatoes, country ham, every kind of onion I've ever seen, any kind of cheese I can get my hands on…you get the idea. I love burgers.

But it starts with the basic, and honestly, no matter how fancy you get, it's hard to beat the classic, all-American cheeseburger. So the first recipe in this book is for exactly that, and we're going to talk about some pretty nit-picky details. I'm going to get picky because like all simple dishes, there are a few techniques that make the dish. You can go all out on the meat, the buns, the ingredients, the seasonings – and yet, if you screw up the technique, you'll get a very mediocre result. The opposite is true as well though – you can have less than stellar ingredients, and have a rock star result, if you know the techniques. So let's talk about those before we even start with a recipe.

Use 85/15 ground beef for burgers. For most recipes I use 90/10, but burgers need the extra fat. A lot will render out on the grill, but burgers need what remains in order to be juicy.

Season correctly! That's rule number one. You need generous kosher salt, and freshly cracked black pepper. The MAIN thing that home cooks miss, and that restaurants get right, is plain old salt. Most home cooks are afraid of salt, and as a result the food just doesn't have any punch. So before you even begin to make the patties, sprinkle the ground beef with a good pinch of kosher salt, and several grinds of black pepper. You'll add more after you make the patties, but you want the inside to taste good too, right? So start with salt and pepper. Now – if you are still keeping it super simple, but want to really boost the beefiness of your burgers, sprinkle very lightly with Worcestershire sauce. Just a tablespoon per pound and you'll notice a world of difference. Feel free to skip it – just using salt and pepper correctly will make the biggest difference – trust me.

To make the patties, divide a pound of beef into the portion size you want. Meaning – four portions makes ¼ pound burgers, which tends to make a good sized burger for a grownup. I often divide a pound into 6 or 8 portions because I have small children, and the portion is more appropriate, and I've made cooking-challenge burgers with 1/3 pound or ½ pound portions. Remember, we're not talking recipe yet, we're talking technique. The easiest way is to simply slightly indent the top of the beef with your hand so that you have a good visual when it's time to divide the beef and make the patties. You want them all the same size so they cook at the same rate – it makes having the burgers come out at the right doneness at the same time much easier. So divide the beef, then gently shape the meat into patties. Don't press too much, they'll be dense and tough. And don't handle the meat more than necessary – again, they'll end up dense and tough. But gently shape the meat into disks, and then press a divot into the top of each patty, making the edges thicker. Burgers shrink as they cook, and the edges of the patties often will crack. The divot helps prevent this. Set the patties aside.

Now break out the salt and pepper again. I like kosher salt, and I teach folks how to use it by telling them to make it 'snow' on top of the food. The nice thing about kosher salt is that it's easy to see the seasoning. But hold your hand well up from the food, and let the salt fall as though it's snowing. Not a blizzard – just snow. Repeat with pepper, and you'll end up with the right amount, correctly distributed over the food. Flip the patties and season the second time with salt and pepper. Now if you want, you can add any additional seasoning you want. If I add anything, I add garlic powder and onion powder (I make a seasoning blend at home that's salt, pepper, onion and garlic powders that I call S.O.S.). But remember, just beef, salt and pepper is delicious. So don't worry about it.

If you'd like, you can wrap the burgers tightly and chill them for a bit. Not too long – the salt will draw moisture to the surface of the burgers and make getting a crust on them more difficult. Or you can take them straight to the grill or griddle. Either way, these steps will go really far in making some awesome, Bombshell burgers.

All American Cheeseburger

INGREDIENTS

1 ½ pounds ground beef
2 teaspoons kosher salt
1 teaspoon freshly ground black pepper
1 egg, lightly beaten
4 onion rolls
4 slices cheddar cheese
Toppings, sliced onion, tomato, lettuce, dill pickle slices, ketchup, mayo, mustard

DIRECTIONS

In a medium bowl, mix ground beef, salt, pepper, Worcestershire sauce and egg. Shape into four patties.

In a large skillet over medium high heat, cook patties about 4-5 minutes per side, for medium well. Place a slice of cheese on top of each patty and cook 1 minute more. Serve on toasted onion rolls with desired toppings.

Cottage Pie

All righty – there are really three things that most folks are referring to when they talk about cottage pies. The first is a shepherd's pie – which is pretty much exactly the same as cottage pie, but made with lamb or mutton, while a cottage pie is made with beef. There's also a Cumberland pie, which again is the same, except topped with cheese and bread crumbs as well as the potatoes. All three dishes are nearly identical, but like with many comfort foods, I've seen people get pretty radical about insisting on the 'authentic' way to make each one, and how they can't be mixed up, and how only the British or Irish or Scots can make them…you know the routine. People get kinda crazy over fried chicken, tacos, beef stew – name your beloved comfort food and people will argue about it.

I've read that cottage pies were named as early as 1790, and that they were called such because they involved lots of potatoes. Meaning they were cheap and therefore appealing to people who lived in cottages, since they'd be poor. Shepherd's pie, using lamb, didn't appear in print for almost another hundred years. Apparently the name was differentiated since shepherds were involved with sheep instead of cattle. Whatever the case, both dishes ended up as beloved in the US as they are in the UK.

I usually don't make a batch of mashed potatoes to make cottage pie, I simply double a batch for dinner some night then use it a day or two later to top cottage pie. It's also a great way to stretch ground beef. Although the recipe calls for a pound a half, you can cut that in half, and increase the amount of veggies to make up the difference in volume.

INGREDIENTS

For the potatoes:

1 ½ pounds potatoes – I like russet potatoes, peeled and diced
2 teaspoons kosher salt
¼ cup half and half
2 tablespoons butter
½ teaspoon kosher salt
½ teaspoon freshly cracked black pepper
1 egg yolk

For the filling:

2 tablespoons olive oil
1 onion, chopped
2 carrots, diced
3-4 cloves garlic, finely minced
1 ½ pounds ground beef
1 teaspoon kosher salt
1 teaspoon freshly cracked black pepper
3 tablespoon four
1 tablespoon tomato paste

1 cup chicken or beef broth
1 teaspoon Worcestershire sauce
1 teaspoon rosemary, minced
3-4 sprigs fresh thyme, minced
½ cup corn kernels
½ cup peas

DIRECTIONS

1. Preheat oven to 400F.

Place the diced potatoes in a medium saucepan and cover with cold water. Add 2 teaspoons kosher salt. Bring to a boil, reduce to a simmer, and cook until very tender, about 15 minutes. Drain.

2. Return potatoes to the saucepan, add butter and half and half, salt and pepper, and mash well, making sure seasonings are well mixed. Add the egg yolk and stir just until combined.

3. Heat the olive oil in a medium skillet over medium heat. Once hot, sauté the onion and carrot until they begin to soften, about five minutes. Add the garlic and cook until fragrant, another 2 minutes. Add the ground beef, salt and pepper and cook until all pink is gone.

5, Sprinkle the contents of the skillet with the flour, stirring well until the flour is thoroughly combined. Add the tomato paste, Worcestershire sauce, rosemary and thyme, and stir well. Bring to a boil, reduce to a simmer, and cover. Simmer for about 10 minutes, or until sauce has thickened. Remove from heat and stir in corn and peas.

6. Transfer mixture to a large casserole dish. Beginning at the edges, top the dish with the mashed potatoes. Bake for 25 minutes, or until the top of the potatoes are golden brown. Allow dish to rest for 15 minutes before serving.

Shepherd's Pie with Potato Crust

INGREDIENTS

FILLING

1 ½ pounds ground beef
2 tablespoons olive oil
1 cup red wine
1 tablespoon tomato paste
3 tablespoons butter
1 onion, chopped
2 carrots, chopped
3-4 garlic cloves, minced
3 tablespoons all-purpose flour
2 cups beef broth
1 tablespoon Worcestershire sauce
1 tablespoon fresh rosemary, chopped
1 teaspoon fresh thyme, chopped
2 teaspoons kosher salt
1 teaspoon freshly ground black pepper
1 ½ cups fresh or frozen English peas
3-pounds potatoes, peeled and sliced very thin
2 tablespoons butter, melted
2 tablespoons chopped fresh flat-leaf parsley

DIRECTIONS

Preheat oven to 375F. Lightly grease a 9x13 casserole dish.

In a large skillet over medium heat, brown ground beef, stirring to crumble, until fully cooked. Drain excess grease. Add wine and tomato paste and cook until wine is fully evaporated, about 5 minutes. Remove from skillet and set aside.

To the same skillet, add butter, onion and carrots. Sauté for about 5 minutes, or until onions are tender. Add garlic and sauté another 30 seconds. Stir in flour and stir to fully combine. Stir in broth, bring to a boil and reduce to a simmer. Simmer for 10 minutes.

Stir in Worcestershire sauce, rosemary, thyme, salt and pepper. Stir in peas and beef and remove from heat.

Place potato slices and ¼ cup water in a microwave safe bowl. Cover with plastic wrap and microwave for 5 minutes on high. Arrange about 2/3 of the potato slices in the casserole dish, overlapping them slightly, covering the bottom and sides. Spoon meat mixture into the potato crust and top with remaining slices of potato. Brush with melted butter.

Bake for 45 minutes, or until potatoes are tender. Turn on broiler, and broil for about 3 minutes until potato crust is golden brown and crispy. Allow casserole to rest 10 minutes before sprinkling with fresh parsley and serving.

Cabbage Rolls

The majority of cabbage rolls are made with a sauce that's as sweet as it is sour. This one is simply a bit sour – I've really been working to get all of the sugar out of my kids' diets, and much of that is having them become much less accustomed to the sugar that seems to be in almost everything we eat. But– if you want the traditional style cabbage rolls, then just add ½ cup brown sugar to the sauce.

Another healthy move you can make with this recipe is to use either quinoa or brown rice. White rice is what we all grew up with, but if you make the swap to brown you'll have more of the nutrients that come with whole grains, and less of the starchy elements of the highly refined white rice. But again, use what you like – it's your food, make it the way you love it!

INGREDIENTS

1 tablespoon kosher salt
1 large green cabbage, 2-3 pounds
2 tablespoons butter
1 large onion, finely chopped
2-3 garlic cloves, minced
2 cups cooked rice
½ pound ground beef
½ pound ground pork
2 teaspoons kosher salt
2 teaspoons oregano
2 teaspoons freshly cracked black pepper

1 green bell pepper, very finely chopped
2 stalks celery, including leaves, finely chopped
2 large cans (28-ounces) tomato sauce or crushed
tomatoes
2 tablespoons cider vinegar
½ cup sour cream, plus more for serving

DIRECTIONS

Remove the core of the cabbage with a paring knife. Fill a large stockpot with enough water to submerge the head of cabbage, add about 1 tablespoon of kosher salt, and bring to a boil. Add the cabbage, cook for about 2 minutes and remove cabbage from the pot. Carefully peel off the outer leaves, return the cabbage to the boiling water. Repeat the cooking and removing of out leaves until all the leaves are softened.

Trim the thick center stem from the bottom of each leaf. Line the bottom of a Dutch oven with the largest leaves.

In a large skillet, melt butter over medium heat. Add onion and garlic, and cook until translucent and fragrant, about 5-7 minutes. Remove from heat. In a large mixing bowl, combine the onion/garlic mixture, rice, beef, pork, salt, pepper, oregano, bell pepper and celery. Mix well.

Place about 1/3 of a cup of the ground beef mixture in the center of one cabbage leaf. Fold the sides of the cabbage leaf over the filling. Working from the stem end, roll the cabbage up. Repeat, transferring the rolls to the Dutch oven as you work.

In a large bowl combine the tomatoes or tomato sauce with the vinegar. Pour sauce over cabbage rolls until almost covered. Place Dutch oven on medium high heat. Bring to a boil, reduce to a simmer and cover. Cook for about an hour, or until cabbage is very tender.

Place sour cream in a small bowl. Add about ½ cup of the tomato sauce from the cooked cabbage rolls, and mix well. Pour sour cream sauce over the cabbage rolls. Serve with additional sour cream.

Sloppy Joes

INGREDIENTS

2 ½ pounds ground beef
1 green bell pepper, diced
1 large onion, diced
1 cup water
1 ½ cups ketchup
5-6 cloves garlic, finely minced
2 tablespoons brown sugar
1 tablespoon chili powder
1 teaspoon dry mustard
1 teaspoon red pepper flakes
1 teaspoon tabasco sauce
2 teaspoons Worcestershire sauce
1 teaspoon kosher salt
½ teaspoon freshly ground black pepper
8 hamburger buns
Sliced dill pickles, for serving

DIRECTIONS

In a large skillet over medium heat, brown the ground beef until no more pink shows. Drain fat.

Add the bell pepper, onion and garlic and cook until fragrant, about 5 minutes. Add water and ketchup, and stir well. Add brown sugar, chili powder, mustard, red pepper, hot sauce, Worcestershire, salt and pepper.

Reduce heat so the mixture is just at a simmer, cover and cook for 20 minutes. Taste and adjust for seasoning. Serve on hamburger buns. These are great with sliced dill pickles.

Easy Cheesy Tacos

INGREDIENTS

1-pound ground beef
1 onion, chopped
1 teaspoon olive oil
1 tablespoon chili powder
2 teaspoons ground cumin
1 teaspoon kosher salt
1 (15-ounce) can pinto beans, rinsed and drained
1 (8-ounce) can tomato puree
¾ cup water
½ cup salsa
6-ounces Cheddar cheese, shredded
1 tablespoon chopped fresh cilantro
Taco shells or tortillas, warmed
Toppings: shredded lettuce, diced tomatoes, diced onion, salsa, sour cream

DIRECTIONS

In a large skillet over medium-high heat, cook beef, stirring well until the beef crumbles and no pink shows. Drain well and set beef aside.

In the same skillet, heat olive oil. Sauté onion for about five minutes. Stir in chili powder, cumin, salt and ground beef. Cook another five minutes or so.

Stir in beans, tomato puree, water and salsa. Mash some of the pintos with a fork. Bring skillet to a boil, reduce the heat to a simmer, and simmer, uncovered, 10 minutes or until the liquid has reduced.

Top beef mixture with cheese. Turn off heat, cover and let stand for about 5 minutes for cheese to melt. Sprinkle with cilantro. Serve on taco shells or tortillas, and top with lettuce, diced tomatoes, diced onion, salsa or sour cream.

Beef Breakfast Sausages

Although we're used to pork sausages at breakfast, sausages were traditionally made by butchers with a variety of meats. Some of the finest sausages in the world hail from Germany and France and contain beef. This recipe is super simple, and takes only a few minutes to throw together. Make enough for a couple of days, then just cook them up as you need them!

INGREDIENTS

1 tablespoon brown sugar
2 teaspoons dried sage
2 teaspoons kosher salt
2 teaspoons dried basil
1 teaspoon ground black pepper
1 teaspoon onion powder
1 teaspoon freshly cracked black pepper
½ teaspoon dried marjoram
¼ teaspoon crushed red pepper flakes
2-pounds ground beef

DIRECTIONS

In a small bowl, stir together all the seasonings. Place ground beef in a large bowl and sprinkle evenly with the spice blend. Working with your hands, mix until the spices are thoroughly distributed throughout. Cover and chill overnight to let the flavors marry.

Divide the mixture into 8 even portions, and form into patties.

Spray a large skillet with cooking spray. Heat oven medium heat, and cook the patties about 6-7 minutes per side, until golden brown and cooked through.

Salisbury Steak

I love this stuff. My grandmother made Salisbury Steak, and it's one of my favorite comfort food dishes. It was originally created by a Dr. Salisbury after the Civil War, and was 'prescribed' three times a day to treat infirm Civil War soldiers.

INGREDIENTS

For the 'steaks':

1 ½ pounds ground beef, 80/20 or leaner
½ cup dry breadcrumbs, seasoned
1 tablespoon ketchup
2 teaspoons dry mustard
4 dashes Worcestershire sauce
1 teaspoon garlic powder
1 teaspoon onion powder
1 teaspoon kosher salt
1 teaspoon freshly cracked black pepper
1 tablespoon butter
1 tablespoon olive oil

For the gravy:

1 onion, diced
2 cups beef broth
1 tablespoon ketchup
1 teaspoon garlic powder
1 teaspoon onion powder

1 teaspoon Worcestershire

1 teaspoon cornstarch

1 teaspoon kosher salt

1 teaspoon freshly cracked black pepper

DIRECTIONS

For the 'steaks', combine the ground beef, breadcrumbs, ketchup, dry mustard, Worcestershire, garlic and onion powders, salt and pepper. Mix well, and form into oval patties. You can make between 4 (they'll be huge) and 8 (much smaller, great for little ones).

In a large skillet, heat the butter and olive oil. Cook the patties on medium until cooked through, about 7-8 minutes per side. Remove from heat and set aside. Drain the skillet.

Return the skillet to medium heat. Add onions and sauté for 5-7 minutes, until softened and fragrant. Add the cornstarch to the beef broth, then add it to the skillet. Stir in ketchup, garlic and onion powders, Worcestershire, salt and pepper. Bring up to a simmer, and return patties to the skillet, turning to coat patties with the gravy. Simmer for 1-2 minutes, or until sauce is thickened and patties are hot through.

Greek Baked Ziti

INGREDIENTS

12-ounces ziti pasta
1 onion, chopped
1 tablespoon olive oil
2 garlic cloves, minced
1 ½ pounds ground beef
2 (15-oz.) cans tomato puree
1 tablespoon lemon juice
1 ½ teaspoons oregano
¼ teaspoon cinnamon
1 ½ teaspoons kosher salt, divided
3 tablespoons butter
3 tablespoons all-purpose flour
3 cups milk
1 cup Parmesan cheese, grated
½ teaspoon freshly ground black pepper
cooking spray
8-ounces mozzarella cheese, grated
1/3 cup dry breadcrumbs

DIRECTIONS

Preheat oven to 350F. Cook pasta according to package directions in salted, boiling water.

While the pasta cooks, heat olive oil over medium high heat. Sauté onions until fragrant, about 5 minutes. Add garlic, and sauté another minute. Add ground beef, stirring until crumbled, and cook until no longer pink. Drain fat.

Stir in tomato sauce, lemon juice, oregano, cinnamon and 1 teaspoon kosher salt. Stir well. Bring to a boil, reduce to a simmer, and cook for a couple of minutes, stirring occasionally. Remove from heat.

In a large saucepan over medium low heat, melt the butter. Add flour and cook, whisking constantly, for 2-3 minutes. Slowly whisk in milk. Increase heat, and cook, whisking constantly for 5 minutes or until thickened. Stir in Parmesan, pepper and remaining salt. Add sauce to pasta, tossing to coat well.

Lightly spray a 9x13 inch baking dish with cooking spray. Transfer pasta to the casserole dish and top with beef mixture. Sprinkle with mozzarella, then breadcrumbs.

Bake at 350F for 25 minutes, or until pasta is bubbly and cheese is melted. Allow the dish to rest for 10-15 minutes before serving.

Hamburgers Diane

Steak Diane is one of my favorite dishes – I absolutely adore it. But it's a bit out of my price range, especially is I want to serve it to my family. Good steaks are high, and that adds up pretty quickly. But you can capture all the flavors of the restaurant classic at a fraction of the price, using the same wonderful ingredients with ground beef instead of steak. I like crimini mushrooms for the flavor, and I tend to grab merlot for sauces, but use what you like best, or swap the wine for beef broth. You'll love the results either way.

INGREDIENTS

1 ½ pounds ground beef

2 ½ teaspoons Worcestershire sauce, divided

1 teaspoon onion powder

1 teaspoon garlic powder

1 teaspoon kosher salt

1 teaspoon freshly cracked black pepper

2 Tablespoons butter, divided

¼ cup shallot, finely chopped

4-ounces button or crimini mushrooms, chopped

¼ cup red wine

1 tablespoon Dijon

1 tablespoon lemon juice

½ cup heavy cream

2 teaspoons chives, minced

DIRECTIONS

In a large bowl, combine the ground beef with 1 teaspoon of the Worcestershire sauce, onion and garlic powders, salt and pepper. Form into 4, 1-inch-thick patties.

In a large skillet over medium heat, melt the butter. Cook patties on each side about 5 minutes, or until browned. Remove from skillet and set aside.

Add remaining butter to the skillet. Sauté shallots and mushrooms for about 5-6 minutes, or until softened and the onion is fragrant.

Add red wine. Stir, scraping up the browned bits from the bottom of the pan. Reduce for 1-2 minutes. Add Dijon mustard, lemon juice, remaining Worcestershire sauce and cream. Bring up to a bare simmer. Taste and adjust for salt and pepper.

Return beef patties to the skillet, along with any juices, turning to coat with the sauce. Cook for another 1-2 minutes or until hot through. Sprinkle with chives and serve with the sauce.

Dirty rice

I've said before that nothing goes to waste in my kitchen. That's a hallmark of the Southern Appalachian style of cooking, and dirty rice is a dished that evolved from cooks with the same mindset. Traditionally, dirty rice was a means by which to make use of the chicken giblets and liver that otherwise would have possibly been thrown out. The 'dirty' color of the rice is from the liver – it turns the rice a nice, rich brown. Today it's very often made with pork or beef as well as with giblets.

I've made dirty rice for years the way my grandmother made it, with chicken liver and giblets as the meat component, and my kids loved it. It wasn't until a couple of months ago, when I told my oldest son that I had ground beef and asked what he wanted for dinner, that I realized there was quite a disconnect. He, and the other kids, just assumed the dish was made with beef. I didn't tell them that they'd been eating liver and giblets for years – that kind of revelation has back fired on me in the past (I.e. my youngest will eat 'sea chicken' but not salmon). No I just didn't say a word. I developed this recipe using beef and ground pork, and just keep serving liver when I have it. Shhhh….

One note – you can use any combination of beef, pork, liver and giblets you like, as long as your total combination equals a pound. Use what you have on hand – that's the nature of the dish. And I'm going to vent for a minute – yes, dirty rice is most common in southern Louisiana, but the dish has been made all over the South for centuries. What makes it authentic isn't the exact ingredients of the dish, but the spirit of stewardship involved in not wasting ingredients. My grandmother's family passed this dish to me, and they've been in the Appalachians for centuries. Which makes mine as authentic as it gets. So – there's my rant. Don't let anyone fuss at you over the authenticity of your food. It's YOURS.

INGREDIENTS

2 cups uncooked rice
4 cups chicken stock
4 cloves garlic, finely minced
1 onion, diced
1 green bell pepper, diced
2 tablespoons olive oil
1 teaspoon kosher salt
1 teaspoon freshly cracked black pepper
1 teaspoon thyme
1 bay leaf
¼ to ½ teaspoon cayenne pepper
¼ pound bulk pork sausage
¼ pound ground beef
½ pound chicken giblets
1 bunch green onions, including the green tops, minced

DIRECTIONS

In a fine strainer, rinse the rice under cold water several times, until the water runs clear. Place rice in a large saucepan and add the chicken stock. Bring to a boil, reduce to a bare simmer and cover. Simmer for 20 minutes and remove from heat. Set aside.

Meanwhile, in a large skillet, heat the olive oil. Sauté garlic, onion and bell pepper until softened, about 7-9 minutes. Sprinkle with salt and pepper. Add thyme, bay leaf and cayenne pepper and add mixture to the rice.

Return skillet to the heat, increase it to medium and cook the beef and sausage together, stirring to crumble, until no more pink shows and the meats are cooked through. Add beef and sausage to the rice.

Meanwhile, in a separate pot, place giblets over medium heat. Add enough water to cover, bring to a boil, reduce to a simmer, and simmer for about 30 minutes. Drain, and allow to cool until cool enough to handle. Finely chop giblets, sprinkle with salt and pepper and add them to the rice.

Return rice to medium low heat. Stir together all ingredients, and cook for about ten minutes, stirring constantly, until flavors marry. Stir in green onion and serve.

One Pot Spaghetti and Meat Sauce

I often make giant batches of <u>marinara</u>, and use it for several meals. It can be used alone, then as a base for cabbage rolls, stuffed peppers, meat sauce, Bolognese, lasagna…It's one of the most rewarding recipes I have as far as time invested and delicious dishes that are the return. But one occasion I like just throwing everything in one pot and being done. This recipe is perfect for that. The sauce and pasta cook in one pot, and the result is fabulous. A full flavored, meaty sauce and perfectly cooked pasta. One pot to wash, and dinner is on the table in under an hour. Bombshell.

INGREDIENTS

1-pound ground beef
1 large onion, chopped
3-4 garlic cloves, minced
1 8-ounce can tomato sauce
1 6-ounce can tomato paste
3 cups tomato juice (use V-8 for a more mellow, complex flavor)
1 cup water
1 teaspoon kosher salt
2 teaspoons dried basil
2 teaspoons dried oregano
1 teaspoon freshly cracked black pepper
1 7-ounce package spaghetti, uncooked
To finish, grated Parmesan, freshly minced parsley

DIRECTIONS

In a <u>Dutch oven</u> over medium heat, cook ground beef, stirring to crumble until meat is no longer pink. <u>Drain</u> excess fat. Add onion and garlic, and cook for five minutes, until vegetables are fragrant. Stir in tomato sauce, tomato paste, tomato juice, water, salt, basil, oregano, and pepper. Stir well. Bring to a boil, reduce to a simmer and cover. Cook, stirring often, ½ hour.

Add pasta. Cover and simmer again, stirring often, 20 minutes, or until pasta is tender. To serve, sprinkle with parmesan cheese and parsley.

Homestyle Meatloaf

This is the simplest meatloaf I know. Only a few ingredients, and just 1 pound of ground beef, it throws together in moments then finishes in the oven. Make sure you use leaner ground beef, at least 85/15. I use 90/10 and get nice results. If you wish, you can form the loaf and bake it on a rack – the excess grease will drain away, although the meatloaf itself will be more dry.

INGREDIENTS

2 eggs, beaten
½ cup ketchup
½ cup milk
1 cup bread crumbs, seasoned
      Or bread crumbs plus
      1 teaspoon oregano
      1 teaspoon kosher salt
      ½ teaspoon black pepper
½ cup finely chopped onion
1 lb. ground beef
To glaze:
¼ cup ketchup

DIRECTIONS

Preheat oven to 350F.

In a large mixing bowl, combine all ingredients, mixing thoroughly but only until the ingredients are combined. Overmixing can make the meatloaf tough.

Place mixture into a 8x4 loaf pan. Bake for 40 minutes.

Remove meatloaf from the oven. Spread ¼ cup ketchup over the top. Return to the oven, and bake an additional 20 minutes until meatloaf is cooked through and ketchup has glazed on the top. Allow meatloaf to rest at least 10 minutes before serving.

Beef and Macaroni

INGREDIENTS

1 ½ pounds lean ground beef
1 large onion, chopped
½ green bell pepper, finely chopped
2 cloves garlic, minced
2 15-ounce can diced tomatoes
1 teaspoon kosher salt
1 teaspoon black pepper
2 teaspoons Cajun spice mix
1 teaspoon paprika
1 bay leaf
2 cups macaroni
½ cup sour cream
3-4 green onion, minced, including green tops

DIRECTIONS:

In a Dutch oven, brown ground beef, stirring frequently to crumble meat until brown and no longer pink. Drain excess grease. Add onion, bell pepper and garlic to Dutch oven, and cook, stirring frequently, about five minutes, or until vegetables are tender. Stir in tomatoes, salt, pepper, chili powder, paprika and bay leaf, and cook, stirring occasionally, about 20 minutes.

Meanwhile, in a separate pot of lightly salted boiling water, cook macaroni according to package directions. Drain and set aside.

Discard bay leaf from the sauce. Stir hot, cooked macaroni into sauce and stir to fully coat pasta. Cook for an additional 5 minutes. To serve, sprinkle with green onion and serve with sour cream.

Beef and Cheese Manicotti

INGREDIENTS

1 8-ounce package uncooked manicotti shells
½ pound bulk Italian sausage, hot or mild
½ pound ground beef
1 onion, chopped
½ cup white wine, such as pinot gris
2 cups cream
2 teaspoons dried Italian seasoning
2 teaspoons kosher salt
1 teaspoon pepper
1 14 ½ -ounce can diced tomatoes, drained
2 cups 8 ounces shredded mozzarella cheese
¾ cup shredded Parmesan cheese

DIRECTIONS

Preheat oven to 350F.

Cook pasta shells according to package directions. Drain and set aside.

Cook sausage and ground beef over medium heat in a large skillet, stirring until meats are crumbled, and no pink shows. Drain excess fat from the skillet. Add onion and cook for about 5 minutes, or until onion is fragrant. Remove meat mixture from the skillet and set aside in mixing bowl.

Add wine to the skillet, scraping at the bottom with a wooden spoon to loosen the browned bits. Bring to a boil. Add cream, Italian seasoning, salt and pepper. Simmer, stirring occasionally until thickened, about 15 minutes. Remove from heat and set aside.

Add tomatoes and mozzarella cheese to the meat mixture. Spoon mixture into cooked pasta shells and layer into a lightly greased 9x13 casserole dish. Cover tightly with foil.

Bake for 20 minutes at 350F. Remove foil and pour cream sauce evenly over shells and sprinkle with Parmesan cheese. Bank, uncovered, for an additional 10 minutes. Turn oven to broil, and broil 3 minutes or so, until cheese is golden brown. Allow dish to rest 10 minutes before serving.

Mexican Lasagna

INGREDIENTS

2-pounds ground beef
3 tablespoons taco seasoning
½ onion, chopped
1 15-ounce can black beans, drained
1 14-oz can fire roasted tomatoes
1 cup corn kernels
Kosher salt
8 8-inch flour tortillas
2 ½ cups Cheddar or pepper jack, shredded
4 green onions, finely chopped, including green tops

DIRECTIONS

Preheat oven to 425F.

In a large skillet over medium heat, brown ground beef, stirring frequently to crumble beef. Cook until no pink shows, about 5 minutes. Drain excess grease.

Add onion, and cook until fragrant, about five minutes. Add taco seasoning and stir well. Add tomatoes, black beans and corn, and stir well. Cook another 2-3 minutes, just until hot through. Taste and adjust for salt.

Lightly grease a 9x13 casserole dish. Cut the tortillas into quarters to make them easier to layer. Start with a layer of meat, then tortillas, then cheese. Repeat in that order, meat layer, tortilla layer, cheese layer until all ingredients have been used.

Bake for 15 minutes at 425, until cheese is golden brown and bubbly. Allow casserole to rest for 5 minutes before cutting. Sprinkle with green onions to serve.

Southwestern Meatloaf

Over the past few years, I have figured out how to make more and more of my own 'mixes' and sauces at home. I make my own salsas, taco seasoning, Italian seasoning – you name it. You don't have to – it does take a few minutes to make the chipotle salsa in this recipe. If you are pressed for time, go ahead and use bottled salsa. You can even use plain tomato salsa if you can't find the chipotle variety – it's still delicious. But I love the smoky heat of chipotle chilies, and if you have the time and can find the ingredients, try making it from scratch. I think you'll be pleasantly surprised – and immediately hooked.

INGREDIENTS

½ cup finely crushed whole grain tortilla chip crumbs
1 teaspoon cumin
1 teaspoon garlic powder
½ teaspoon freshly ground black pepper
1 cup chipotle salsa
1 tablespoon chipotle salsa
1 teaspoon kosher salt
½ teaspoon kosher salt
1 ¾ pounds ground beef
1 ½ cups shredded sharp Cheddar cheese
2 large eggs
2 tablespoons ketchup
2 teaspoons fresh lime juice

DIRECTIONS

Preheat oven to 350F.

In a small <u>bowl</u>, stir together tortilla chip crumbs, cumin, garlic powder, pepper, 1 cup salsa, and 1 teaspoon kosher salt. Set aside, and allow to sit for about 10 minutes, stirring on occasion.

In a large bowl combine salsa mixture with ground beef, cheddar and eggs. Combine well but only until just incorporated, don't over mix or your meatloaf will be tough. Shape into a 9x5 inch loaf. Cover a cooking <u>sheet</u> with foil, lightly oil the foil and place loaf on cooking <u>sheet</u>.

Bake for 50 minutes at 350F. Meanwhile, in a small mixing bowl stir together ketchup, lime juice, 1 tablespoon salsa, and remaining kosher salt. Pour evenly over meatloaf, and bake another 15-20 minutes, until glaze sets and meatloaf is cooked through. Allow meatloaf to rest for at least 10 minutes before serving.

Swiss Burgers in Tomato Gravy

Simmer ground sirloin patties in a rich tomato gravy to create luscious fork-tender burgers. Serve with steamed green beans.

INGREDIENTS

1 teaspoon kosher salt
1 ½ pounds ground beef
1 large egg, lightly beaten
1 teaspoon ground black pepper
1 onion, sliced
2 15-ounce can fire-roasted diced tomatoes
1 teaspoon Worcestershire sauce
½ cup water
6-ounces Swiss cheese, sliced
2 tablespoons fresh basil, chopped

DIRECTIONS

In a large bowl, combine ground beef, eggs, salt and pepper. Mix just until fully combined. Divide mixture into six portions and shape into patties.

In a large skillet over medium high heat, cook patties about 5 minutes on each side until nicely browned. Remove patties from the skillet and set aside. In the same skillet, sauté onion for about 3 minutes or until beginning to get fragrant. Add tomatoes, Worcestershire sauce and water. Bring to a boil and reduce to a simmer. Simmer for five minutes.

Return beef patties to the skillet, turning to coat with the sauce. Turn heat to medium low. Cover skillet and cook for about 15 minutes. Uncover and simmer an additional 5 minutes. Cover each patty with a slice of the Swiss cheese. Cover and cook just until cheese melts. Sprinkle with fresh basil and serve.

Beef and Tomato with Polenta Crust

Don't laugh, but for the longest time I didn't have a clue what polenta was. Then I figured out it's nothing more than cornmeal – which I of course grew up with. I immediately embraced it – it's just a close cousin of grits. Grits are ground more coarsely, but everything else about it is pretty much the same. Which means - you can make this with grits if you want. It's wonderful, especially if you can find stone ground grits. This is just a comforting, friendly, delicious dish – your family will love this one.

INGREDIENTS

1 teaspoon kosher salt
3 cups water
1 cup plain yellow cornmeal
½ teaspoon Montreal steak seasoning
1 cup shredded sharp Cheddar cheese, divided
1-pound ground beef
1 onion, chopped
1 medium zucchini, sliced
1 tablespoon olive oil
2 15-ounce cans petite diced tomatoes, drained
1 can tomato paste
2 tablespoons fresh parsley, chopped

DIRECTIONS

Preheat oven to 350F.

In a large saucepan over medium high heat, bring water and kosher salt to a boil. Whisk in cornmeal, reduce heat to low and simmer, whisking constantly, about 3-4 minutes, or until thickened. Remove from heat. Stir in steak seasoning and half the cheddar cheese. Spread mixture in the bottom of a lightly greased 11x7 casserole dish.

In a large skillet over medium heat, brown ground beef, stirring frequently to crumble, until meat is no longer pink. Drain excess grease and transfer beef to a separate bowl.

In the same skillet, add olive oil, and sauté onion and zucchini for about 5 minutes, or until just tender, but still crisp. Stir in beef, tomatoes and tomato paste. Bring to a boil, reduce to a simmer, and cook for about 10 minutes. Transfer beef and tomato mixture to the casserole over the cornmeal. Sprinkle with remaining cheese.

Bake for 30 minutes or until bubbly, and cheese is golden brown and gooey. Allow casserole to rest for 10 minutes. Sprinkle with fresh parsley and serve.

Jamaican Beef Patties

These are just incredible, and for the authentic version, use Scotch Bonnet. Now listen – a scotch bonnet will take your head off if you aren't careful, so use gloves when working with it. If you can't find them, or if you need a lower heat level, substitute jalapeno pepper, which is still spicy, but not nearly at the level of a scotch bonnet. If you want the medium heat level, go with a serrano pepper. I use serrano, since the scotch bonnets I planted haven't come in yet, and they're hard to find here. But the 'real' version uses the real thing. So pick your heat level and enjoy!

INGREDIENTS

For the pastry:

2 cups all-purpose flour
1 ½ teaspoons curry powder
½ teaspoon kosher salt
¼ cup shortening
4 tablespoon butter, cold
1/3 cup ice water

For the filling:

2 tablespoons butter
1 onion, finely chopped
¼ teaspoon Scotch bonnet pepper (authentic and very spicy)

Or 1 small minced jalapeno (less spicy) or serrano pepper (medium high heat)

½ pound ground beef

½ teaspoon curry powder

½ teaspoon dried thyme

½ teaspoon allspice

1 teaspoon kosher salt

1 teaspoon freshly cracked black pepper

¼ cup breadcrumbs

¼ cup beef stock

¼ cup water

1 egg, lightly beaten

DIRECTIONS

For the pastry:

Add the flour, curry powder and salt in the bowl of a food processor. Pulse to combine. Add shortening and butter, and pulse in bursts until mixture is crumbly. Add ice water and pulse just until the dough comes together.

Roll dough on a floured surface to 1/8 inch thick. Let rest for about 15 minutes. Cut out 10 circles 8 inches in diameter. Cover with plastic wrap until ready to fill.

For the filling:

In a heavy skillet over medium heat, brown ground beef, stirring until crumbly, until no longer pink. Set beef aside and drain excess grease.

In the same skillet, melt butter and sauté onion and chili pepper until softened, about 5 minutes. Add back the beef and stir in curry powder, thyme, allspice, salt and pepper. Stir well.

Stir in breadcrumbs and beef stock. Cover, and allow to simmer for about 10 minutes, stirring occasionally, or until liquid is absorbed. Remove from heat and allow to cool for about 10-15 minutes.

Preheat oven to 400F. Lightly grease baking sheet.

Place 3 tablespoons of the filling in the center of each pastry disk. Mix remaining water with the beaten egg. Moisten the edges of the circles, fold in half, and crimp edges with a fork. Brush the tops of the pastries with the egg wash.

Bake about 35 minutes or until golden brown. Allow pastries to rest for at least 10 minutes before serving.

Simple, Perfect Chili

I keep the ingredients for this chili in the pantry all the time, and it's easy to just throw together and let simmer for a few minutes. Supper in no time, and it's perfectly delicious. I often make a double batch, and use the extra for making Walking Tacos, Chili Bowls or Chili Topped Potatoes. And of course it makes perfect lunches the next day. You can even throw this into a slow cooker and let it go. This is a go-to you'll love!

INGREDIENTS

1 ½ pounds ground beef
1 onion, chopped
1 green bell pepper, chopped
3-4 cloves garlic, minced
1 jalapeno pepper, stemmed, seeded and finely chopped (optional)
2 16-ounce cans kidney beans, drained and rinsed
2 15-ounces cans diced tomatoes
3 tablespoons chili powder
2 teaspoons kosher salt
1 ½ teaspoons cracked black pepper
1 ½ teaspoons cumin

DIRECTIONS

In a large skillet over medium heat, brown ground beef, stirring occasionally to crumble. Cook until no longer pink. Drain excess grease. Add onion, bell pepper, garlic and jalapeno. Cook for about 5 minutes. Stir in remaining ingredients, bring to a boil, reduce to a simmer, and simmer, uncovered, for about an hour.

Chili Topped Potatoes

This chili makes a big batch, so feel free to stash the extra in the freezer for a second meal in no time!

INGREDIENTS

1-pound ground beef

1 onion, chopped

1 16-ounce can pinto beans, drained and rinsed

1 15-ounce can corn, drained

2 15-ounce cans diced tomatoes, undrained

1 4.5-ounce can green chilies, undrained

2 tablespoons taco seasoning

1 1-ounce packet ranch dressing mix

2 cups water

4 large russet potatoes

To serve, shredded cheddar cheese, sour cream, diced tomatoes, diced green onion

DIRECTIONS

In a Dutch oven, brown ground beef, stirring often until beef is crumbled and no pink shows. Drain excess grease. Stir in pinto beans, corn, tomatoes, chiles, taco seasoning, dressing mix and water. Bring to a boil, reduce to a simmer, and simmer, uncovered, about 20 minutes, stirring occasionally.

Meanwhile, prick potatoes all over with a fork. Microwave on high for about 14-15 minutes, occasionally turning the potatoes as they cook. Let rest for 2-3 minutes before splitting them open. Alternatively, you can bake them for 1 hour at 350 degrees in a regular oven.

Split potatoes, and top with chili. Serve with cheese, tomatoes, sour cream and green onions.

Walking Tacos

INGREDIENTS

1-pound ground beef
2 tablespoons taco seasoning
¼ cup water
4 small packets (2.5 ounces) corn chips
2 cups lettuce, shredded
1 Roma tomato, diced
1 cup shredded Cheddar cheese
1/3 cup salsa
½ cup sour cream

DIRECTIONS

In a large skillet over medium heat, brown ground beef, stirring occasionally to crumble, until cooked through and no longer pink. Drain excess grease. Add taco seasoning and water and simmer for about 10 minutes.

Before opening bags of chips, gently press on the bags to break them up. Carefully open the bags along the edge with scissors. Spoon in beef mixture, lettuce, tomato cheese, salsa and sour cream on top of the broken chips. Serve in the bags.

Chili Bowls - Petro's

INGREDIENTS

2 cups Simple, Perfect Chili
4 small packets (2.5 ounces) Frito corn chips
2 cups lettuce, shredded
1 cup shredded Cheddar cheese
1/3 cup salsa
½ cup sour cream
4 green onions, minced
Hot sauce

DIRECTIONS

Open the Fritos bags by carefully slicing along the side with scissors. Spoon in chili, lettuce, cheese, salsa and sour cream on top of the broken chips. Sprinkle in green onion. Serve in the bags with hot sauce.

Smothered Enchiladas

INGREDIENTS

3 tablespoons olive oil

1 ½ tablespoon flour

¼ cup chili powder

2 cups chicken stock

1 10-ounce can tomato puree

2 teaspoons dried oregano

1 teaspoon cumin

1 teaspoon kosher salt

3 cups shredded cheddar cheese

1-pound ground beef

1 onion, diced

10 corn tortillas

1 cup sour cream

2 tablespoons lime juice

5-6 green onions, diced, including green tops

DIRECTIONS

Preheat oven to 350 degrees F.

In a medium saucepan over medium heat, heat the 3 tablespoons of olive oil. Whisk in flour and cook for one minute. Add chili powder and whisk well. Whisk in chicken stock, tomato puree, oregano, and cumin. Bring to a boil, reduce to a simmer and cook for about 15 minutes. Taste and adjust for salt and pepper, and remove from heat.

In a large skillet over medium heat, brown ground beef, stirring occasionally, until no longer pink, about 5 minutes. Remove from heat, drain excess grease, and stir in cheese and onion.

In a second skillet, heat ½ cup of oil until shimmering. Using tongs, dip the tortillas, one at a time, to soften. Drain on towels. Dip each tortilla in the sauce and place on a plate. Place a generous spoonful of filling on the tortilla and roll up. Place seam side down in a casserole dish and repeat. Top with the remaining sauce.

Bake at 350F for 30 minutes. In a small bowl mix sour cream and lime juice. Serve enchiladas with the lime sour cream sauce and sprinkle with green onions.

Spaghetti with Meat Sauce

INGREDIENTS

1 ½ pounds lean ground beef
1 large onion, chopped
½ green bell pepper, finely chopped
3-4 cloves garlic, minced
2 15-ounce cans crushed tomatoes
1 8-ounce can tomato sauce
1 tablespoon dried Italian seasoning
1 ½ teaspoon kosher salt
1 teaspoon black pepper
2 teaspoons dried basil
12-ounces spaghetti

DIRECTIONS

In a large pot of lightly salted boiling water, cook spaghetti per package directions. Drain.

Meanwhile, in a Dutch oven, brown ground beef, stirring frequently to crumble meat until brown and no longer pink. Drain excess grease. Add onion, bell pepper and garlic to Dutch oven, and cook, stirring frequently, about five minutes, or until vegetables are tender. Stir in tomatoes, salt and pepper, basil and Italian seasoning and cook, stirring occasionally, about 20 minutes.

Add cooked pasta to <u>Dutch oven</u> with the sauce, tossing to coat well.

Beef and Cheese Ravioli Bake

INGREDIENTS

1-pound lean ground beef
1 small onion, diced
8-ounces fresh mushrooms, sliced
1 teaspoon olive oil
3-4 garlic cloves, minced
6 cups marinara sauce
1 cup water
1 tablespoon dried Italian seasoning
1 teaspoon kosher salt
1 teaspoon freshly cracked black pepper
1 20-ounce package refrigerated four cheese ravioli
1 cup shredded mozzarella cheese

DIRECTIONS

Brown ground beef in a Dutch oven over medium heat, stirring occasionally to crumble, and no longer pink. Drain excess grease and set beef aside.

Heat olive oil in same Dutch oven. Sauté onion and mushrooms for about 5 minutes. Add garlic and sauté an additional minute. Stir in beef, marinara, water, Italian seasoning, salt and pepper.

Bring sauce to a boil and add ravioli. Reduce heat to a simmer, cover and simmer for about 10 minutes, stirring occasionally, until pasta is done. Stir in mozzarella and serve.

Hamburger Steak with Mushroom Onion Gravy

INGREDIENTS

1-pound ground beef
1 egg
¼ cup bread crumb
1 teaspoon freshly cracked black pepper
1 teaspoon kosher salt
1 teaspoon onion powder
1 teaspoon garlic powder
1 teaspoon Worcestershire sauce
1 tablespoon olive oil
1 onion, thinly sliced
4-ounces mushrooms, sliced
2 tablespoons all-purpose flour
1 cup beef broth
1 tablespoon sherry
1 teaspoon kosher salt
½ teaspoon freshly cracked black pepper

DIRECTIONS

In a large bowl, mix together the ground beef, egg, bread crumbs, pepper, salt, onion and garlic powders, and Worcestershire sauce. Diving into 8 equal portions, and form into patties.

In a large skillet over medium heat, heat the olive oil. Cook the patties about 5 minutes on the first side. Flip, add onions and mushrooms to the pan, and cook patties another five minutes on the second side. Remove the patties to a plate.

Sprinkle the flour over the onions and stir in, mixing well and scraping up browned bits from the bottom of the pan. Slowly stir in beef broth and sherry. Cook for about five minutes, stirring occasionally, until gravy thickens. Reduce heat to low.

Return patties to the pan, turning to coat. Simmer for 15 minutes, and serve.

Perfect Party Meatballs

Makes about 24 meatballs

INGREDIENTS

1 cup pitted black olives

½ small red onion, coarsely chopped

¾ cup coarsely chopped fresh mint leaves

½ cup coarsely chopped fresh parsley

2 teaspoons lemon zest, about 1 lemon

¾ cup panko breadcrumbs

½ cup ricotta cheese

2 large eggs

2 teaspoons kosher salt

1 teaspoon freshly ground black pepper

1-pound ground beef

1-pound bulk Italian sausage

1 small can tomato paste

3 cups beef broth

1/3 cup hot pepper jelly

2 tablespoons minced fresh parsley

DIRECTIONS

Preheat oven to 450°

In the bowl of a food processor, place olives, onion, mint, parsley and lemon zest. Pulse a few times until ingredients are coarsely chopped.

In a medium bowl, mix breadcrumbs, ricotta, eggs, salt, pepper, beef, sausage and olive mixture. Mix until combined. Shape into one inch meatballs and place on foil lined baking sheets.

Bake at 450F for about 12-14 minutes, or until golden brown.

While meatballs bake, heat a saucepan over medium heat. Add tomato paste to the dry pan and cook, 2-3 minutes, until tomato paste begins to brown. Increase heat to medium high and whisk in beef broth, scraping up the tomato paste from the bottom of the pan. Whisk in pepper jelly and reduce heat to low. Add cooked meatballs, sprinkle with fresh parsley and serve.

Cocktail Meatballs

I buy mostly generic foods – 99% of the time the quality is just as good as the name brands. Gingersnaps are the exception. For some reason I've never found a store brand I like, and the difference is huge. So get the good ones – you'll be glad you did. These meatballs take a few minutes, but they're so worth it.

Makes about 50 meatballs

INGREDIENTS

1 ½ -pounds ground beef
¼ cup dry, seasoned breadcrumbs
2 teaspoons horseradish
2 garlic cloves, minced
¾ cup tomato juice
2 teaspoons kosher salt
1 teaspoon freshly ground black pepper
2 medium-size yellow onions, finely chopped, divided
2 tablespoons butter
2 tablespoons all-purpose flour
1 ½ cups beef broth
½ cup red wine, such as Merlot
2 tablespoons brown sugar, packed
2 tablespoons ketchup
1 tablespoon lemon juice
3 gingersnaps, crumbled

DIRECTIONS

Preheat oven to 450F.

Stir together ground beef, breadcrumbs, horseradish, garlic, tomato juice, salt, pepper and half of the diced onion. Mix just until combined. Don't over mix or the meatballs could be tough. Shape into one inch balls, and place on a lightly greased foil lined baking sheet. Bake for 12-14 minutes, or until golden brown and cooked through.

Meanwhile, in a large skillet over medium heat sauté remaining onions for about 5 minutes, or until fragrant and tender. Whisk in flour, and cook for about a minute. Whisk in beef broth and whisk until smooth. Stir in wine, brown sugar, ketchup, lemon juice and crushed cookies. Reduce heat to low and simmer for 15 minutes, stirring occasionally. Add cooked meatballs, and cook an additional five minutes, stirring gently on occasion.

Greek Burgers with Tzatziki Sauce

INGREDIENTS

For the tzatziki sauce:

6-ounces plain Greek yogurt
¼ cup cucumber, diced
2 tablespoons red onion, minced
1 tablespoon fresh dill
2 teaspoons lemon juice
1 clove garlic, minced

For the burgers:

1-pound ground beef
1 cup feta cheese, crumbled
1/3 cup red onion, chopped
1 tablespoon fresh dill
1 teaspoon kosher salt
1 teaspoon freshly cracked black pepper
2 cloves garlic, finely chopped
4 burger buns
Toppings: thinly sliced tomatoes, lettuce

DIRECTIONS

In a small bowl, stir together ½ cup of the yogurt and the remaining sauce ingredients. Chill until serving.

In a medium mixing bowl, combine all the burger ingredients and ½ cup yogurt. Divide mixture into four equal portions and shape into burger patties.

Place patties on grill or griddle pan over medium heat. Cook for 5 minutes per side, or until cooked through. Serve on burger buns, topped with desired toppings and tzatziki sauce.

Bierocks (German Meat Turnovers)

INGREDIENTS

2 (1-pound) loaves frozen bread dough, thawed
1-pound ground beef
1 onion, chopped
1 clove garlic, crushed
2 teaspoons kosher salt
1 teaspoons pepper
1 teaspoon lemon zest
1 small head cabbage, chopped
2 tablespoons Worcestershire sauce
2 teaspoons caraway seeds
½ cup melted butter

DIRECTIONS

Preheat oven to 350F.

In a large skillet over medium heat brown ground beef, stirring to crumble, until no pink shows. Drain excess grease. Add onion, garlic, salt, pepper and lemon zest and sauté for an additional 5 minutes, or until onion is fragrant and tender. Add cabbage, Worcestershire sauce and caraway seeds. Cook for about 10 minutes or until cabbage is wilted. Drain liquid from mixture.

On a lightly floured surface, roll each portion of dough into a 12-inch circle. Cut each circle into a 6-piece wedge. Divide the filling evenly, and place filling in the center of each dough wedge. Pull the points of the dough up and pinch together to seal. Place bierocks on a lightly greased baking sheet and brush with melted butter.

Bake in preheated oven for 30 minutes, or until golden brown.

Meatballs Stroganoff

INGREDIENTS

1-pound ground beef
1 medium onion, very finely chopped, divided
3 garlic cloves, minced
1 ½ teaspoon kosher salt
1 teaspoon freshly ground black pepper
½ cup fresh bread crumbs
2 large egg yolks
½ cup water
2 tablespoons extra virgin olive oil
½ pound mushrooms, thinly sliced
½ cup dry sherry
2 cups chicken broth or beef broth
2 tablespoons unsalted butter, room temperature
2 tablespoons all-purpose flour
2 tablespoons chopped fresh dill
½ cup sour cream
Additional kosher salt and freshly ground black pepper
to taste

DIRECTIONS

Combine the ground beef, half of the onion, garlic, salt,
pepper, breadcrumbs egg yolks and water in a large.
Mix thoroughly, but don't over mix or your meatballs
may be tough. Shape mixture into meatballs about 1
inch in diameter.

In a large skillet over medium high heat, heat the olive oil. Add the meatballs, working in batches if necessary, and brown them on all sides, about 5 minutes. Remove meatballs from skillet and set aside.

Remove all but 3 tablespoons of fat from the skillet. Add remaining onion, and sauté until onions are fragrant, about 5 minutes. Add mushrooms and cook, stirring until the liquid has evaporated, about 10 minutes.

Add sherry and bring to a boil. Add chicken broth and bring to a simmer.

In a small bowl combine the flour and butter. Mash together until they form a smooth paste. Working with tiny pieces, add the butter/flour mixture to the simmering broth, whisking constantly, until sauce thickens, about 5 minutes. Add meatballs, dill, sour cream, and simmer just until meatballs are heated through. Taste, adjust for salt and pepper and serve.

Spaghetti Pie

INGREDIENTS

For the crust:

7 oz uncooked vermicelli or spaghetti
1 egg
½ cup grated Parmesan cheese

For the filling:

1-pound ground beef
½ cup chopped green bell pepper
¼ cup chopped onion
2 cloves garlic, minced
2 cups marinara sauce

For the topping:

¼ cup cream cheese
½ teaspoon garlic powder
1 cup shredded mozzarella cheese
2 tablespoons chopped fresh basil

DIRECTIONS

Preheat oven to 350F.

In a large pot of lightly salted water, cook spaghetti according to package directions.

Lightly grease a 9-inch, deep dish pie plate.

In a large bowl beat the egg. Add Parmesan cheese and add the cooked pasta, tossing to coat. Spoon mixture into the pie plate, pushing up at the sides to form a crust.

In a large skillet over medium heat, brown ground beef, stirring occasionally to crumble, until no pink shows. Drain excess grease and add bell pepper and onion to the pan. Sauté for about 5 minutes, and add marinara sauce. Stir well.

Spoon beef mixture into the pie plate over the crust. In a small bowl mix together the topping ingredients. Drop topping by rounded teaspoons over the filling.

Bake for 30 minutes until hot through and crust is golden brown. Let stand 10 minutes, cut into wedges, sprinkle with fresh basil and serve.

Old-Fashioned Meatloaf

This Southern meatloaf recipe features Creole and Greek seasonings and a hint of garlic. A few tablespoons of Worcestershire sauce spice up the traditional ketchup topping.

INGREDIENTS

1 tablespoon butter
3 celery ribs, finely chopped
½ large onion, finely chopped
2-pounds lean ground beef
2 tablespoons Worcestershire sauce, divided
½ cup Italian breadcrumbs
1/3 cup ketchup
2 teaspoons Creole seasoning
1 teaspoon Greek seasoning
1 teaspoon garlic powder
2 large eggs, lightly beaten
1 8-ounce can tomato sauce
3 tablespoons tomato paste
1 tablespoon ketchup
Garnish: chopped fresh flat-leaf parsley

DIRECTIONS

Preheat oven to 350F. Line a baking sheet with foil.

Melt butter in a large skillet over medium heat. Add celery and onion, and sauté 5 minutes or just until tender.

Stir together celery mixture, ground beef, half the Worcestershire sauce, breadcrumbs, ketchup, Creole seasoning, Greek seasoning, garlic powder and eggs. Shape into a 10- x 5-inch loaf and place on a baking rack. Set rack on the foil lined baking sheet.

Bake at for 45 minutes. Stir together remaining Worcestershire sauce, tomato sauce, tomato paste, and 1 tablespoon ketchup. Pour over meatloaf, and bake 10 to 15 more minutes or until no longer pink in center. Let stand at least 10 minutes before slicing.

Mini Pepper Relish Meatloaves

I first fell in love with pepper relish when I was living in Seattle, and loved the range of flavors and heat levels. It's also beautiful – jars of pepper relish look like little jewels. It pairs wonderfully with meats of all kinds, and makes the most wonderful glaze for these little meatloaves. I also love miniature meatloaves – they're just so cute.

INGREDIENTS

½ cup fresh breadcrumbs
¼ cup spicy V-8 juice
¼ cup buttermilk
1 onion, minced
1 tablespoon olive oil
1 ¾-pounds ground beef
¼ cup finely chopped fresh basil
1 large egg, lightly beaten
1 tablespoon Dijon mustard
2 teaspoons kosher salt
1 teaspoon freshly ground black pepper
1 cup hot pepper relish, divided
2 tablespoons chopped fresh basil

DIRECTIONS

Preheat oven to 450F.

In a small <u>bowl</u> stir together the bread crumbs, V-8 juice and buttermilk. Set aside.

In a large <u>skillet</u> over medium heat, heat olive oil. Sauté onion for about 5 minutes or until fragrant and tender.

In a large bowl, mix together bread crumb mixture, onion, ground beef, basil, egg, Dijon, salt, pepper and 2 tablespoons of the pepper relish just until combined. Don't over mix or your meatloaves could be tough.

Divide mixture into 8 equal portions and shape each into loaves. Lightly grease a wire rack and place it over a foil lined baking tray. Arrange the loaves on the rack.

Bake at 450F for 20 minutes. Remove from the oven and brush the tops with 1/3 cup of the pepper jelly. Bake an additional 10 minutes. Remove from the oven, and allow to rest for 5 minutes. Serve by sprinkling with chopped fresh basil and with the remaining pepper relish.

Tex-Mex Meatballs in Red Chile Sauce

INGREDIENTS

1 poblano pepper
1 onion, chopped
4 garlic cloves
½ cup firmly packed fresh cilantro leaves
½ cup finely crushed corn chips
¼ cup milk
2 large eggs
2 teaspoons kosher salt
1 teaspoon freshly ground black pepper
2-pounds ground beef
2 ½ cups enchilada sauce
2 cups chicken broth
1 cup sour cream
1 teaspoon lime zest
2 tablespoons fresh lime juice
6-inch corn tortillas, warmed

Toppings: Cotija cheese, radishes, toasted shelled pumpkin seeds (sold as pepitas), cilantro, diced avocado

DIRECTIONS

Preheat broiler. Slice the tops off the poblanos, and remove the seeds, stems and ribs. Slice them in half and lay them flat on a foil lined baking sheet. Broil poblano peppers until blistered, turning occasionally. Place the peppers in a Ziploc bag and let sit for about 10 minutes to loosen the skin. Peel the poblanos and place in the bowl of a food processor.

Add onion, garlic and cilantro to the food processor. Pulse several times until everything is coarsely chopped.

Preheat oven to 400F.

In a large bowl mix together corn chips and milk. Allow to soften for about 5 minutes. Stir in eggs, salt, pepper and poblano mixture. Mix in ground beef, gently but thoroughly. Shape into 1 ½ inch meatballs and place on a foil lined baking sheet.

Bake for about 12-14 minutes or until well browned. Transfer meatballs to a Dutch oven. Add enchilada sauce and broth. Bring to a boil, reduce to a simmer and simmer about 20 minutes or until sauce is slightly thickened, gently stirring to turn meatballs occasionally.

Meanwhile, whisk together sour cream, lime zest and lime juice in a small bowl. Taste and adjust for salt. Serve on tortillas, and accompany with the sour cream and toppings.

Three Cheese Beef Pasta Shells

INGREDIENTS

24 uncooked jumbo pasta shells

1-pound ground beef

4 cups marinara

¼ cup water

8-ounces cream cheese

3 tablespoons chives, minced

1 ½ cups shredded mozzarella cheese

½ cup grated Parmesan cheese

1 egg

2 tablespoons chopped fresh parsley

DIRECTIONS

Preheat oven to 350F.

In a large pot of lightly salted water, cook shells as per package directions.

In a large skillet over medium heat, cook ground beef until no longer pink, about 5 minutes, stirring occasionally to crumble. Drain excess grease and set aside.

In a large bowl, mix marinara sauce and water. Place about 1 cup of the sauce in the bottom of a 9x13 inch casserole dish.

In a medium mixing bowl, mix together the cream cheese, mozzarella cheese, Parmesan cheese, egg and ground beef. Spoon mixture into shells and arrange in the baking dish. Pour remaining sauce over the top and cover with foil.

Bake for 45 minutes. Remove foil, sprinkle with remaining cheese and bake an additional 10 minutes. Sprinkle with parsley and serve.

World's Best Lasagna

INGREDIENTS

1-pound bulk Italian sausage
¾ -pound ground beef
1 onion, finely diced
4 cloves garlic, crushed
1 28-ounce can crushed tomatoes
2 6-ounce cans tomato paste
2 6.5-ounce cans canned tomato sauce
½ cup water
2 teaspoons dried basil leaves
½ teaspoon fennel seeds
1 teaspoon Italian seasoning
1 ½ tablespoon kosher salt
¼ teaspoon ground black pepper
4 tablespoons chopped fresh parsley
12 lasagna noodles
2 cups ricotta cheese
1 egg
1 teaspoon salt
¾-pound mozzarella cheese, sliced
¾ cup grated Parmesan cheese
4 tablespoons fresh minced basil

DIRECTIONS

In a Dutch oven over medium heat, brown sausage and ground beef, stirring occasionally until browned and no longer pink, about 5 minutes. Drain excess grease. Add onion and garlic and sauté an additional 5 minutes.

Stir in crushed tomatoes, tomato paste, tomato sauce, water, basil, fennel seed, Italian seasoning, 1 tablespoon of the salt, pepper, and 2 tablespoons fresh parsley.

Stir in crushed tomatoes, tomato paste, tomato sauce, and water. Season with sugar, basil, fennel seeds, Italian seasoning, 1 tablespoon salt, pepper, and 2 tablespoons parsley. Bring to a boil, reduce to a simmer, and simmer for between 1-2 hours.

After sauce has simmered, bring a large pot of lightly salted water to a boil. Cook noodles according to package directions. Once cooked, set aside on a plastic wrapped baking sheet.

Preheat oven to 375F.

In a large mixing bowl, combine ricotta cheese, egg, remaining parsley and remaining salt.

Place about 1 ½ cups of sauce in the bottom of a 9x13 inch baking dish. Place 6 noodles over sauce, and spread half the cheese mixture over noodles. Top with 1/3 of the mozzarella. Repeat the layers and cover tightly with foil.

Bake at 375F for 30 minutes. Remove foil and bake an additional 30 minutes. Allow to rest for at least 15 minutes before cutting. Sprinkle with fresh basil and serve.

Railroad Pie

INGREDIENTS

1-pound ground beef
1 onion, chopped
1 12-ounce cans whole kernel corn
½ green bell pepper, chopped
1 can tomato soup
1 ¼ cups water
1 tablespoon chili powder
1 teaspoon kosher salt
¾ cup cornbread mix
1 egg
1 tablespoon oil

DIRECTIONS

In a large skillet over medium heat, brown ground beef, stirring occasionally to crumble, until brown and no longer pink, about 5 minutes. Drain excess grease. Add onion and sauté another 5 minutes, until onions are tender and fragrant.

Stir in corn, green pepper, soup, water, chili powder and salt. Bring to a boil, reduce to a simmer and simmer for 15 minutes.

Preheat oven to 350F. Pour mixture into a 9x13 inch casserole dish. In a small bowl mix together the cornmeal mix, egg and oil. Pour over the top of the casserole.

Bake for 20 minutes or until topping is golden brown.

Mince and Tatties

This recipe took some doing, since I had to rewrite an original Scottish recipe for American measurements. The results are wort the effort, it's easy to see why it's such a comfort food in Scotland. I have no idea why this dish hasn't really crossed over here, because it's absolutely incredibly. Probably the sheer stupendous volumes of butter and cream in the potatoes. I ran the math, then actually went online to double check it thinking it couldn't be that much. But yes, yes it is. Scots could be Southerners. ;-) The rich, beefy mince is also gorgeous – especially when topped with the fresh peas.

INGREDIENTS

For the mince:

2-pounds ground beef
3 large onions, chopped
4 cups beef broth
1 teaspoon sea salt
Ground white pepper
½ cup diced carrots, optional
2 teaspoons Worcestershire sauce
½ cup fresh or frozen peas

DIRECTIONS

In a large skillet over medium heat, brown ground beef, stirring occasionally to crumble, until no longer pink and fully browned. Drain excess grease.

Add onions to the skillet, and sauté for 5 minutes or so or until onions are fragrant and tender. Sprinkle with salt and pepper, add carrots if using, add Worcestershire sauce and reduce heat to low and allow to cook for 10 minutes, stirring occasionally.

Add beef stock and bring to a boil. Reduce to a simmer, and simmer, stirring occasionally for about 2 hours. If the mince becomes too dry, add a bit more stock. If too wet just cook it a bit longer. If using peas, stir them in.

Taste and adjust for salt and pepper. Serve with the mashed potatoes.

For the tatties:

8 russet potatoes, peeled and diced
1 ½ sticks butter
1 cup cream
1 tablespoon fresh chives, finely chopped
2 teaspoons sea salt
1 teaspoon freshly ground black pepper

DIRECTIONS

Bring a large pot of salted water to a boil. Add potatoes, reduce pot to a simmer, and simmer for 10-15 minutes, or until potatoes are fork tender. Drain and return potatoes to very low heat for just a few minutes to ensure they are very dry.

Mash by hand or pass the potatoes through a ricer. Add butter and stir in. Add cream ¼ cup at a time until the potatoes reach the desired consistency, which should be very creamy. Stir in chives, salt and pepper. Taste and adjust for seasoning.

Spaghetti Bolognese

INGREDIENTS

¼ cup olive oil
1 onion, chopped
3-4 cloves garlic, chopped
1 stalk celery, chopped
1 carrot, peeled and chopped
1-pound ground beef
1 28-ounce can crushed tomatoes
¼ cup parsley, chopped
¼ cup fresh basil, chopped
1 teaspoon kosher salt
1 teaspoon freshly cracked black pepper
¼ cup parmesan cheese
Fresh basil, for serving

DIRECTIONS

In a large skillet over medium high heat, heat the olive oil. Add garlic and onions and sauté until onions are very soft, about 8-10 minutes. Add the carrots and celery and sauté an additional 5 minutes.

Add ground beef and sauté until meat is cooked through and no pink shows, about 10 minutes.

Stir in tomatoes, parsley and basil. Cook over medium heat, stirring occasionally, until sauce thickens, about 30 minutes. Season with salt and pepper. To serve, ladle over noodles and sprinkle with fresh basil.

Asian Ground Beef, Pepper and Onion Sauté

INGREDIENTS

1-pound ground beef
3 bell peppers, thinly sliced – use red, yellow, and green
1 onion, thinly sliced
3-4 cloves garlic, thinly sliced
2 tablespoons ginger, grated
2 tablespoons parsley
½ teaspoon red pepper flakes
1 teaspoon salt
1 cup beef broth
3 tablespoons soy sauce
1 tablespoon unsulfured molasses
1-1 teaspoons chili paste
1 teaspoon Worcestershire sauce
¼ cup water
2 tablespoons cornstarch
4 green onions, sliced thin

DIRECTIONS

In a large skillet over medium heat, cook the ground beef, stirring occasionally to crumble, until no long pink. Drain excess grease, remove beef from skillet and set aside.

Return the heat to the stove, turning heat up to medium high. Add the peppers, onion, garlic and ginger, parsley, red pepper and salt. Sauté, stirring frequently, until tender, about 5 minutes. Return the beef to the skillet.

In a small bowl, stir together beef broth, soy sauce, molasses, chili paste and Worcestershire sauce. Add sauce to skillet and bring to a boil.

In a small bowl, combine water and cornstarch to skillet, stirring constantly until sauce thickens. Serve over rice and sprinkle with green onions

Korean Beef Rice Bowls

INGREDIENTS:

For the beef:

¼ cup soy sauce
2 teaspoons brown sugar, packed
1 teaspoon sesame oil
½ teaspoon red pepper flakes
2 teaspoons olive oil
1-pound ground beef
½ onion, diced
2 garlic cloves, minced
2 teaspoons grated ginger

For the bowls:

3 cups cooked brown rice
1 cucumber, unpeeled, skin on
2 tablespoons Go Chu Jong
½ tablespoon sesame seeds
3-4 green onions, including green tops, sliced

DIRECTIONS

In a small bowl, stir together the soy sauce, water, brown sugar, sesame oil and red pepper flakes.

In a very large skillet over medium high heat, cook ground beef, stirring occasionally to crumble until cooked through and no pink shows. Drain any excess grease, and add onion, garlic and ginger. Sauté for 1 minutes. Pour sauce over the beef. Bring to a boil, reduce to a simmer and cover. Simmer for 10 minutes.

To serve, place ¾ cups rice in each bowl. Top with beef, cucumbers, additional go chu jong if desired, sesame seeds and green onions.

Asian Beef and Cabbage Salad

INGREDIENTS

1-pound ground beef
¼ cup plum sauce
1/3 cup rice vinegar
3 tablespoons olive oil
1 teaspoon kosher salt
1 teaspoon freshly cracked black pepper
4 cups shredded Napa cabbage
4 green onions, including green tops, thinly sliced
2 large carrots, cut into thin strips
1 cup cilantro, minced

DIRECTIONS

In a large skillet over medium heat, cook ground beef, stirring to crumble, until browned and no longer pink. Stir in plum sauce.

Meanwhile, in a mixing bowl, whisk the vinegar, oil, salt and pepper together. Add cabbage, green onions, carrots and cilantro, and toss to thoroughly coat with the dressing. Top with beef mixture and serve.

Mediterranean Beef Pitas

INGREDIENTS

1-pound ground beef
2 teaspoons dried oregano
1 teaspoon kosher salt
1 teaspoon freshly cracked black pepper
1 tablespoons olive oil
4 pocketless pitas
¾ cup hummus
¼ small red onion, sliced
2 tablespoons fresh parsley
1 lemon, cut into wedges

DIRECTIONS

Divide the beef into 4 patties, and season with oregano, salt and pepper on both sides.

Heat the oil in a large skillet over medium heat. Cook patties about 4 minutes per side in the hot oil.

Place patties on the pitas, and top with hummus, onion, parsley. Serve with lemon wedges.

Korean Ground Beef Egg Rolls

INGREDIENTS

1-pound ground beef
1 tablespoon sesame oil
3-4 cloves garlic, minced
1 ½ teaspoons fresh ginger, minced
½ cup brown sugar
¼ cup soy sauce
½ tablespoon Sriracha (or to taste)
24 egg roll wrappers
10 leaves Napa cabbage, torn into small squares
2 carrots, cut into matchsticks
Oil, for frying

DIRECTIONS

In a large skillet over medium heat, brown the ground beef, stirring well to crumble until brown and no longer pink. Drain excess oil. Add sesame oil, garlic and ginger and cook for 1 minute. Add brown sugar, soy sauce and Sriracha. Cook until the liquid has reabsorbed. It should be shiny, but no soupy. Remove meat from pan and set aside.

Return pan to the heat. Add carrots and sauté for about 4 minutes, or until just softened. Allow to cool until cool enough to handle.

Lay egg roll wrappers on work surface. Top each wrapper with a square of the Napa cabbage. Top with 5-6 carrot sticks and 2 tablespoons of the beef. Using your finger, wet all four sides. Fold two sides over the filling and dampen the folded sides. Roll each wrapper closed and set aside. Place the rolled rolls on a baking sheet and freeze.

To cook, heat oil to 350F. Fry each egg roll for about 4 minutes. Drain on a wire rack and serve.

Ground Beef Bulgogi

INGREDIENTS

1-pound ground beef
1 tablespoon olive oil
3-4 cloves garlic, minced
1 teaspoon fresh ginger, minced
2 tablespoons brown sugar
¼ cup soy sauce
1 tablespoon sesame oil
½ teaspoon red pepper flakes
1 teaspoon kosher salt
1 teaspoon freshly cracked black pepper
3 green onions, including green tops, thinly sliced
1 tablespoon sesame seeds

DIRECTIONS

In a large skillet over medium heat, brown the ground beef, stirring well to crumble until brown and no longer pink. Drain excess grease. Add garlic and ginger and sauté for 1 minute. Add brown sugar, soy sauce, sesame oil, red pepper flakes, salt and pepper. Sauté for about 5 minutes.

Remove from heat, stir in green onions and sesame seeds. Serve hot with rice.

Asian Inspired Ground Beef

INGREDIENTS

1-pound ground beef
3-4 cloves garlic, minced
½ onion, minced
3 green onions, including green tops, thinly sliced
½ cup coconut sugar
¼ cup tamari
1 tablespoon sesame oil
½ teaspoon red pepper flakes
1 teaspoon fresh ginger, grated
Cooked rice or lettuce leaves for serving
3 tablespoons fresh cilantro, chopped

DIRECTIONS

In a large skillet over medium heat, brown the ground beef, stirring well to crumble until brown and no longer pink. Drain excess grease.

Meanwhile, whisk together coconut sugar, tamari, sesame oil, red pepper and ginger.

To the ground beef, add onion and garlic and sauté for about five minutes. Add sauce, and cook, stirring often for about 3 minutes. Remove from heat.

Add green onions and cilantro, and serve with rice or in lettuce leaves.

Sesame Garlic Beef Tacos

INGREDIENTS

8 corn tortillas
1-pound ground beef
2 tablespoons toasted sesame oil
2 cloves garlic, minced
½ teaspoon crushed red pepper flakes
¼ cup soy sauce
3 tablespoons brown sugar, packed
3 tablespoons rice vinegar
1 tablespoon water
Quick Pickled Cucumbers and Cabbage (recipe below)
Lime wedges
Sriracha

DIRECTIONS

Preheat oven to 350F. Wrap tortillas in foil and warm for 10 minutes.

Meanwhile, in a large skillet over medium heat, brown ground beef, stirring to crumble, until no longer pink, about 5 minutes. Drain excess grease and set the beef aside.

To the same skillet, add sesame oil and garlic. Cook for 1 minute. Add red pepper, soy sauce, brown sugar, vinegar and water. Bring to a boil, reduce to a simmer and simmer for 5 minutes, stirring occasionally. Add beef back to the skillet and stir well until hot through.

To serve, spoon beef mixture into tortillas, top with pickled cucumbers and cabbage. Pass lime wedges and Sriracha.

Quick Pickled Cucumbers and Cabbage

INGREDIENTS

¼ cup rice vinegar

2 tablespoons sugar

1 teaspoon kosher salt

1 cup cucumber, halved, seeded, and very thinly sliced

1 cup finely shredded red cabbage

DIRECTIONS

In a medium bowl, whisk together vinegar, sugar and salt. Add cucumber and cabbage and toss well to combine. Chill for at least 15 minutes before serving.

Eastern European Kotlety

These are traditionally served with mashed potatoes and applesauce, which makes an incredible comfort food meal.

INGREDIENTS

1 1/3-pounds ground beef

2/3 cups milk crackers, crushed

1 onion, minced

1 egg, beaten

1 tablespoon milk

2 cloves garlic, minced

1 ½ teaspoons kosher salt

1 teaspoon freshly ground black pepper

½ cup shortening, for frying

DIRECTIONS

In a large skillet over medium high heat, melt shortening. Sear patties on each side, about 3 minutes, until golden brown. Reduce heat to medium low, and cook until cooked through, about ten minutes more. Drain on paper towels and serve hot.

Serbian Ground Beef, Veggie, and Potato Bake

INGREDIENTS

1-pound ground beef

1 tablespoon olive oil

1 green bell pepper, chopped

1 onion, chopped

1 carrot, shredded

2 celery stalks, chopped

½ tablespoon paprika

1 teaspoon kosher salt

1 teaspoon freshly cracked black pepper

½ teaspoon crushed red pepper

1 pinch ground cinnamon

1 pinch ground cloves

¼ cup water

2 tablespoons red wine

1 teaspoon Worcestershire sauce

2 tablespoons half-and-half

2 potatoes, peeled and sliced

DIRECTIONS

Preheat oven to 400F. Lightly grease a 9x13 baking dish.

In a large skillet over medium heat, brown ground beef, stirring to crumble, until no longer pink, about 5 minutes. Drain excess grease, and set the beef aside.

In the same skillet, heat olive oil. Sauté green pepper, onion, carrot and celery until just tender, about 5 minutes. Return beef to the skillet. Stir in paprika, salt, pepper, red pepper, cinnamon and cloves. Add water, red wine and Worcestershire sauce. Remove from heat and stir in half and half.

In the bottom of the casserole dish, place a layer of the sliced potatoes. Spoon beef mixture on top of potato layer, and top with remaining potato slices. Bake for 45 minutes, or until hot and bubbly, and the potatoes are tender.

Asian Lettuce Wraps

INGREDIENTS

1 ½-pounds ground beef
1 onion, diced
4 cloves garlic, minced
1 tablespoon minced ginger
1-ounce can water chestnuts, chopped
1/3 cup hoisin sauce
1 tablespoon soy sauce
Lettuce – Bibb or romaine

Toppings: shredded carrot, chopped peanuts, toasted sesame seed, sliced green onion, cilantro

DIRECTIONS

In a large skillet over medium heat, cook ground beef, stirring to crumble, until cooked through and no longer pink. Drain excess grease and set beef aside.

In the same skillet sauté the onion, garlic and ginger for about 3 minutes. Return beef to the pan and add water chestnuts. Stir in hoisin and soy sauces, and allow mixture to simmer for about 5 minutes.

To serve, place the meat mixture in the lettuce cups and top with your choice of toppings.

Simple Taco Soup

INGREDIENTS

2-pounds ground beef
2 tablespoons taco seasoning
1-½ cups water
1 15-ounce can whole kernel corn, drained
2 15-ounce cans pinto beans, rinsed and drained
2 14.5-ounce cans diced tomatoes
2 4-ounce cans chopped green chilies, optional
3 tablespoons (1 envelope) ranch salad dressing mix

DIRECTIONS

In a large skillet over medium heat, cook ground beef, stirring to crumble, until cooked through and no longer pink. Drain excess grease.

Add remaining ingredients and stir well. Bring to a boil, reduce to a simmer, and simmer, about 15 minutes, stirring occasionally.

Poor Man's Beef Wellington

INGREDIENTS

2 eggs, lightly beaten
1 ½ pounds ground beef
¼ cup bread crumbs
4 tablespoons fresh parsley, minced
2 teaspoons kosher salt
1 tablespoon cream
3 tablespoons butter
1 onion, finely chopped
4 gloves garlic, minced
1 8-ounce package mushrooms
½ cup red wine
1 teaspoon basil
mozzarella cheese (optional)
2 sheets of puff pastry
1 egg, lightly beaten
2 sheets puff pastry, thawed

DIRECTIONS

Preheat oven to 400F.

In a large mixing bowl combine eggs, ground beef, bread crumbs, parsley, salt and cream. Mix thoroughly but don't over work the meat or it could become tough. Form into 8 round patties, and set aside.

In a large skillet over medium heat melt butter. Sauté onions and mushrooms until onions are translucent. Add garlic, wine and basil. Stir well and continue cooking until reduced and most of the liquid has reabsorbed.

On a lightly floured surface lay out pastry sheets. Cut each sheet into 4 squares. Divide mushroom mixture evenly among the squares. Add a patty to the top of each square and top with a little mozzarella cheese. Pull the corners of the pastry up around the meat, and pinch to close. Lay each seam side down on a lightly greased cookie sheet.

Cut a small slit on the top of each bundle, and brush with the remaining egg. Bake for about 40 minutes, or until golden brown and the meat is cooked through.

Mexican Pizza

INGREDIENTS

½-pound ground beef
1 onion, diced
2 cloves garlic, minced
1 tablespoon chili powder
1 teaspoon ground cumin
1 teaspoon black pepper
1 teaspoon kosher salt
dash cayenne powder
1 16-ounce can refried beans
4 10-inch flour tortillas
½ cup salsa
2 cups shredded cheese, such as Monterrey Jack, cheddar or mozzarella
2 green onions, including green tops, chopped
8 grape tomatoes, diced
1 small jalapeno pepper, minced
¼ cup sour cream

DIRECTIONS

Preheat oven to 350F. Lightly grease a baking sheet.

In a large skillet over medium heat, cook ground beef, stirring to crumble, until cooked through and no longer pink. Drain excess grease. Add onion and garlic to the pan, and saute 5 minutes or until onion is tender. Stir in chili powder, cumin, salt, pepper and cayenne.

Place two tortillas on the baking sheet and cover each with a layer of refried beans. Scatter half the ground beef mixture over the refried beans, and top with another tortilla. Bake 10 minutes.

Remove from over, and top each with salsa. Add cheese, tomatoes, green onion and jalapenos. Bake an additional 5 minutes, or until cheese has melted. Remove from the oven, allow to cool to set, and cut each into 4 pieces. Serve with sour cream.

Meatball Sub Hot Pockets

INGREDIENTS

1-pound ground beef

½ cup Italian bread crumbs

2 cloves garlic, minced

¼ cup fresh parsley, minced

1 teaspoon red pepper flakes

2 teaspoons kosher salt

1 teaspoon freshly ground black pepper

1 pie crust

½ cup marinara

1 ½ cup mozzarella, shredded

1 egg, beaten with 1 tablespoon of water

DIRECTIONS

Preheat oven to 350F. Line two baking sheets with parchment paper and set aside.

In a large bowl, combine bread crumbs, garlic, parsley, red pepper flakes, salt and pepper. Roll into one inch meatballs, and transfer to baking sheet. Bake for 15 minutes, allow to cool, and cut each into fourths.

On a lightly flour surface, roll pie crust into a large rectangle, squaring the edges with a knife if necessary. Slice into four pieces.

Add marinara, meatballs and mozzarella onto each piece of dough, and fold over. Crimp and seal the edges with a fork. Brush the top of each dough piece with egg wash and transfer to the second baking sheet. Bake for 20 minutes, until golden brown.

Hobo Beans

INGREDIENTS

1-pound ground beef
½ pound bacon, diced
1 28-ounce can baked beans
1 15-ounce can kidney beans, drained and rinsed
1 15-ounce can lima beans, drained and rinsed
2 onions, diced
1 cup ketchup
1 cup brown sugar, firmly packed
2 teaspoons mustard
Kosher salt and freshly cracked black pepper, to taste

DIRECTIONS

In a large skillet over medium heat, cook ground beef and bacon, stirring to crumble the beef, until the beef is cooked through and no longer pink, about 5 minutes. Drain excess grease, and transfer to a slow cooker. Stir in all remaining ingredients. Cook on low 3-4 hours, until thickened.

Cheeseburger Casserole

INGREDIENTS

2 cups uncooked rotini noodles
2 teaspoons olive oil
1 onion, finely chopped
2 cloves garlic, minced
1-pound ground beef
1 teaspoon kosher salt
1 28-ounce can diced tomatoes
2 tablespoons Dijon mustard
2 cups grated cheddar cheese
¼ cup dill pickles, chopped

DIRECTIONS

Preheat oven to 350F. Lightly grease a 9x13 casserole dish. Cook pasta according to package directions in salted boiling water. Drain.

Meanwhile, in a large skillet over medium heat, brown the ground beef, stirring to crumble until cooked through. Drain excess grease.

Return beef to the skillet, add onion and garlic and cook about 5 minutes. Stir in tomato paste, tomatoes and mustard. Bring to a simmer and cook until slightly thickened, about 3 minutes.

Stir pasta into the meat mixture, mixing well. Spoon into the prepared casserole dish. Sprinkle cheddar cheese over the top and bake about 15 minutes, until cheese is fully melted. Sprinkle chopped pickles over the top and serve.

Slow Cooker Beef and Cheese Pasta

INGREDIENTS

2-pounds ground beef

1 onion, diced

2 cloves garlic, minced

4 cups marinara sauce

1 tablespoon Italian seasoning

½ teaspoon crushed red pepper flakes

2 tablespoons Worcestershire sauce

2 beef bouillon cubes

1 teaspoon kosher salt

1 teaspoon freshly cracked black pepper

10-ounces frozen spinach, defrosted and squeezed dry

1-pound uncooked penne pasta

½ cup Parmesan cheese

1 ½ cup mozzarella cheese, shredded

DIRECTIONS

Meanwhile, over medium heat, cook the ground beef, stirring to crumble, until fully cooked and no longer pink. Drain excess grease. Add onions and garlic and cook about 5 minutes.

Transfer onions and beef to a slow cooker. Add marinara sauce, Italian seasoning, red pepper flakes, Worcestershire sauce, bouillon cubes, salt and pepper. Cook on low for 6 to 8 hours.

In a large pot of salted boiling water, cook pasta according to package directions. Drain. Add pasta to the sauce, stirring well to combine. Add Parmesan and mozzarella cheeses, turn heat to high and allow to cook for 30 minutes. Stir in spinach and serve.

Super Nachos

INGREDIENTS

2 bags tortilla chips

For the salsa:

4 tomatoes, seeded and chopped
1 jalapeno pepper, seeded, veined and minced
1 onion, chopped
¼ cup cilantro, finely chopped
2 teaspoons kosher salt

For the topping:

1 tablespoon olive oil
1-pound ground beef
3 cloves garlic, minced
1 onion, chopped
1 jalapeno pepper, seeded, veined and finely chopped
2 teaspoons kosher salt
1 tablespoon chili powder
1 ½ teaspoons tobacco (or more if you like)
1 15-ounce can black beans, drained and rinsed

For the cheese sauce:

2 tablespoons butter
3 tablespoons flour
2 cups milk
1 cup pepper jack cheese, shredded

1 ½ cups cheddar cheese, shredded
Optional Toppings: Sour cream, green onions, black olives, diced avocados

DIRECTIONS

Place tortilla chips on a large platter – the biggest you have, or use a baking sheet.

In a medium bowl, combine salsa ingredients. Set aside.

In a large skillet over medium heat, cook ground beef, stirring to crumble, until cooked through. Drain excess grease. Add garlic, onion and peppers to the beef and sauté about five minutes. Season with salt, chili powder and tobacco. Stir in beans and reduce heat to low.

In a saucepan over medium heat, melt butter. Whisk flour in and cook for about 2 minutes. Slowly whisk in milk, bring up to a simmer, and stir in cheeses.

Spoon meat mixture over the tortilla chips, and pour cheese sauce over the top of the meat. Top with the salsa and any additional toppings and serve immediately.

Porcupine Meatballs

INGREDIENTS

1-pound ground beef

½ cup uncooked rice

½ cup water

½ onion, minced

2 teaspoons kosher salt

½ teaspoon celery salt

1 teaspoon garlic powder

1 teaspoon freshly cracked black pepper

1 15-ounce can tomato sauce

1 cup water, or more if needed

2 teaspoons Worcestershire sauce

DIRECTIONS

In a large mixing bowl, combine the ground beef, rice, ½ cup water, onion, salt, celery salt, garlic powder and pepper. Ross into 12 meatballs.

In a large skillet over medium heat, cook the meatballs, turning occasionally, until browned. Drain excess grease. Add tomato sauce, water and Worcestershire sauce and reduce heat to medium low. Cover and simmer until meatballs are cooked through and rice is tender, about 45 minutes. Add additional water if the sauce begins to get too dry.

Tennessee Meatloaf

INGREDIENTS

For the glaze:

½ cup ketchup
¼ cup brown sugar, packed
2 tablespoons apple cider vinegar

1 tbsp rice wine vinegar

For the meatloaf:

1 onion, diced
½ green bell pepper, diced
3-4 cloves garlic, minced
2 large eggs
1 tablespoon dried thyme
2 teaspoons kosher salt
1 teaspoon ground black pepper
2 teaspoons dry mustard
1 tablespoon Worcestershire sauce
1 teaspoon Tabasco
½ cup milk
2/3 cup oatmeal
2-pounds ground beef

Directions

Preheat oven to 350F. Lightly grease two 9x5 loaf pans, or one 9x13 casserole dish.

In a small bowl, combine ketchup, brown sugar and vinegar. Mix well, set aside.

DIRECTIONS

Combine ketchup, brown sugar, and cider vinegar in a bowl; mix well.

In a large mixing bowl, combine onion, pepper, garlic, eggs, thyme, salt, pepper, mustard, Worcestershire sauce, tabasco sauce, milk and oats. Combine thoroughly. Alternately, you can all these ingredients to the bowl of a food processor and pulse until you have a pretty goopy paste. Either way, you want these ingredients well combined, so you won't have to overwork the meatloaf, which can make it tough.

Once the vegetables and seasonings are well combine, add beef, and mix thoroughly, but don't overmix.

Shape mixture into loaves, and place into the prepared pans, or into one loaf and place in the casserole dish. Spread half the glaze over the top. Bake for 50 minutes. Remove from the oven, and carefully drain off collected fat. Top loaves with the remainder of the glaze, and bake an additional 10 minutes. Allow to rest at least 15 minutes before serving.

Easy Blue Ribbon Chili

INGREDIENTS

2-pounds ground beef

1 onion, chopped

2 cloves garlic, minced

1 teaspoon ground black pepper

2 teaspoons kosher salt

2 teaspoons garlic powder

2 ½ cups tomato sauce

1 cup salsa

4 tablespoons chili powder

2 15-ounce cans kidney beans

DIRECTIONS

In a Dutch oven over medium heat, brown the ground beef, stirring to crumble, until no pink remains. Drain excess grease. Add onion and garlic, and cook about 5 minutes, or until onion is tender.

Add the salt and pepper, garlic powder, tomato sauce, salsa, chili powder and kidney beans. Stir well. Bring to a boil, reduce to a simmer, and simmer for about an hour.

Italian Ground Beef Casserole with Biscuit Topping

INGREDIENTS

1-pound ground beef

1 onion, diced

2 teaspoons kosher salt

1 teaspoon freshly cracked black pepper

¾ cup water

1 8-ounce can tomato sauce

1 6-ounce can tomato paste

2 cups mozzarella cheese, grated

1½ cups frozen peas, carrots and corn

1 can flaky biscuits

1 tablespoon butter, melted

1 ½ teaspoons dried oregano, crushed

DIRECTIONS

Preheat oven to 375F. Lightly grease a 9x13 inch casserole dish.

In a large skillet over medium heat, brown ground beef, stirring occasionally to crumble, until no longer pink. Drain excess grease. Add onion and cook for about 5 minutes, or until onion is tender. Season with salt and pepper.

Stir in water, tomato sauce and tomato paste. Bring to a boil, reduce to a simmer, and simmer for about 15 minutes, stirring occasionally.

Transfer half the beef mixture to the baking dish. Top with half the cheese, and spoon vegetables over the top of the cheese. Top with the remaining beef mixture, and top with remaining cheese.

Pull biscuits in half and place the biscuits over the top of the cheese, overlapping them. Brush melted butter over the biscuit tops, and sprinkle with oregano. Bake for about 30 minutes or until golden brown.

Double Stuffed Taco Potatoes

INGREDIENTS

4 large baking potatoes
1-pound ground beef
1 onion, diced
3 tablespoons taco seasoning
¼ cup water
½ cup sour cream
¼ cup milk
1 cup cheddar cheese, shredded
4 green onions, including green tops, chopped
½ cup salsa

DIRECTIONS

Preheat oven to 400F. Prick potatoes in several places, and bake for 1 hour, or until cooked through.

Meanwhile, brown ground beef over medium heat in a large skillet, stirring to crumble, until no pink shows and beef is cooked through. Drain excess grease. Add taco seasoning and water, cook for an additional minute, and remove from heat. Set aside.

Allow potatoes to cool until cook enough to handle. Remove the skin from just the top of each potato, and scoop out the insides, leaving a small layer of cooked potato inside so the skins don't collapse. Place potato in a large bowl. Add sour cream and milk and mash well.

Stir in the beef mixture and all but ¼ cup of the cheddar cheese. Taste and adjust for salt and pepper.

Spoon potato mixture back into the skins and transfer to a baking dish. Sprinkle with remaining cheese. Bake for about 15 minutes, or until hot through and cheese is melted. Serve with salsa, sour cream and green onions.

Stuffed Spaghetti Squash with Tomato and Ground Beef

INGREDIENTS

1 large spaghetti squash
1-pound ground beef
Half a green pepper, diced
1 onion, diced
3 garlic cloves, minced
1 Portobello mushroom, sliced
1 28-ounce can diced tomatoes, drained
2 teaspoons kosher salt
1 teaspoon freshly cracked black pepper
2 teaspoons fresh thyme leaves, minced
1 teaspoon fresh oregano leaves, minced
½ teaspoon cracked red pepper flakes
¼ cup Parmesan cheese

DIRECTIONS

Preheat oven to 400F.

Pierce spaghetti squash several times with the tip of a knife. Place on a baking sheet and cook for about 40-45 minutes, or until the skin can easily be pierced with a knife. Reduce oven heat to 350F. Cut squash in half, and allow to cool until cool enough to handle. Remove seeds. Run the tines of a fork over the flesh of the squash to create strands resembling pasta.

While squash cooks, in a large skillet over medium heat, brown ground beef until cooked through, stirring to crumble. Drain excess grease. Add onions, garlic, bell pepper and mushrooms, and sauté for about 5 minutes, or until veggies are fragrant and tender.

Stir in tomatoes, salt, pepper, thyme, oregano and red pepper flakes. Bring to a boil, reduce to a simmer and simmer for about 10 minutes.

Spoon sauce over the squash halves and top with Parmesan cheese. Bake for about 10 minutes, or until hot through and cheese is melted.

Cabbage and Ground Beef Soup

INGREDIENTS

1-pound ground beef
1 tablespoon olive oil
1 onion, diced
2-3 cloves garlic, minced
1 teaspoon dried thyme
1 teaspoon dried marjoram
2 teaspoons kosher salt
1 teaspoon freshly cracked black pepper
1 pinch crushed cloves
1 small head cabbage, shredded
2 carrots, diced
2 stalks celery, diced
3 cups beef broth
3 cups water
3 tablespoons tomato paste
2 bay leaves
1 tablespoon Worcestershire sauce
1/3 cup uncooked rice
Lemon slices, for serving

DIRECTIONS

In a large saucepan, cook ground beef over medium heat, stirring to crumble, until cooked through and no longer pink, about 5 minutes. Drain excess grease.

To the same pan, add olive oil. Add onion, garlic, thyme, marjoram, salt, pepper and cloves. Sauté for about 5 minutes, or until onion is tender. Add cabbage, carrots and celery and cook an additional 3 minutes. Add beef broth, water, tomato paste, bay leaves, Worcestershire sauce, ground beef and rice and stir to combine.

Bring to a boil and reduce to a simmer. Simmer, stirring occasionally, until rice is cooked and cabbage is tender. Serve soup with lemon slices.

Ground Beef Noodle Soup Recipe

INGREDIENTS

1 ½ pounds ground beef
1 onion, diced
1 carrot, diced
1 stalk celery, diced
7 cups beef broth
2 bay leaves
2 teaspoons kosher salt
1 teaspoon freshly cracked black pepper
1-1/2 cups uncooked egg noodles

DIRECTIONS

In a large saucepan, brown ground beef, stirring to crumble, for about 5 minutes, or no longer pink and cooked through. Drain excess grease.

Add onion celery and carrot to the beef and cook about 5 minutes, stirring occasionally, until vegetables are tender.

Add beef broth, bay leaves, salt and pepper. Bring to a boil, reduce to a simmer and stir in noodles. Simmer, for 15 minutes, or until noodles are tender.

Easy Stuffed Zucchini

INGREDIENTS

½ pound ground beef
1 zucchini
½ cup bread crumbs
2-3 cloves garlic, minced
2 cups marinara sauce
2 tablespoons black olives, chopped
½ cup Parmesan cheese
1 cup mozzarella cheese

DIRECTIONS

Preheat oven to 350F.

In a large skillet over medium heat, brown ground beef, stirring occasionally, until meat is cooked through and no longer pink, about 5 minutes. Drain excess grease.

Transfer beef to a large mixing bowl.

Trim the ends off zucchini. Slice in half and scoop out the flesh with a spoon, leaving a ½ inch shell all around. Finely chop the zucchini flesh and add to the beef. Stir in bread crumbs, garlic, marinara sauce, olives, and Parmesan cheese. Mix well. Lightly stuff the zucchini with the stuffing mixture. Transfer to a baking dish and cover with foil.

Bake for 45 minutes. Remove foil, and sprinkle mozzarella over each zucchini. Turn oven to broil and move rack to 6 inches below broiler. Broil 3-4 minutes, or until cheese is golden brown and bubbly.

Real Deal Hamburger Helper

INGREDIENTS

1-pound ground beef
1 ½ cups uncooked whole wheat penne
2 cups milk
½ cup water
2 tablespoons flour
1 teaspoon onion powder
1 teaspoon garlic powder
½ teaspoon paprika
2 teaspoons kosher salt
1 cup shredded cheddar cheese

DIRECTIONS

In a large skillet over medium heat, brown ground beef, stirring to crumble, until thoroughly cooked and no longer pink. Drain excess grease. Stir in pasta, spices and flour. Add cheese, milk and water, stirring well. Bring to a boil and reduce to a simmer, stirring occasionally.

Cover and allow to simmer about 15 minutes, stirring occasionally until pasta is tender.

Picadillo Cubano

INGREDIENTS

2-pounds ground beef

2 teaspoons of ground cumin

1 teaspoon of ground oregano

1 bay leaf

1 onion, finely chopped

1 green bell pepper, finely chopped

5 garlic cloves, minced

2 teaspoons kosher salt

1 teaspoon freshly cracked black pepper

1 cup tomato sauce

1 tablespoon tomato paste

1 cup white wine

½ cup olives with pimiento, sliced

1/3 cup raisins

White rice, to serve

Extra virgin olive oil, to serve

DIRECTIONS

In a large saucepan over medium heat, brown ground beef, stirring to crumble, until fully cooked and no longer pink. Drain excess grease. Stir in cumin, oregano, bay leaf, onion, bell pepper, garlic, salt and pepper. Cook about 10 minutes, stirring occasionally.

Add tomato sauce, white wine, olives and raisins. Bring to a boil, reduce to a simmer and cover. Allow to simmer for about 30 minutes, stirring occasionally.

Remove the bay leaf and serve over plain white rice. Drizzle with olive oil.

Swedish Meatballs

INGREDIENTS

2 slices white bread
¼ cup milk
3 tablespoons butter, divided
1 small onion, very finely chopped
2 teaspoons kosher salt
1 ½ pounds ground beef
2 large egg yolks
1 teaspoon freshly cracked black pepper
¼ teaspoon ground allspice
¼ teaspoon freshly grated nutmeg
¼ cup flour
3 cups beef broth
¼ cup heavy cream

DIRECTIONS

Preheat oven to 200F.

Crumble bread and place in a small bowl. Pour milk over bread pieces and set aside.

In a large skillet over medium heat, melt 1 tablespoon of butter. Add onion, and sauté about 5 minutes, until the onions are soft.

In a large mixing bowl, combine the bread and milk, ground beef, egg yolks, kosher salt, pepper, allspice, nutmeg and onions. Mix well to thoroughly combine, but do not overmix.

Form mixture into 1 inch meatballs and place on a baking sheet.

Heat remaining butter in a sauté pan over medium low heat. Cook meatballs until all sides are brown, about 10 minutes. Transfer to a baking dish and keep warm in the slow oven.

Once all meatballs are cooked, decrease heat under the skillet to low. Whisk in flour and cook about 1 minute. Gradually whisk in beef stock, and stir until thickened. Stir in cream and cook another five minutes, without boiling, until sauce has thickened. Pour sauce over meatballs and serve.

Cheeseburger Gnocchi

INGREDIENTS

1 tablespoon butter
1 16-ounce package potato gnocchi
½ pound ground beef
2 teaspoons kosher salt
1 teaspoon freshly cracked black pepper
2 teaspoons cumin
1 teaspoon smoked paprika
1 teaspoon mustard powder
1 cup onion, chopped
3-4 cloves garlic, minced
1 ½ cups diced tomatoes and chilies
1 cup beef broth
¼ cup heavy cream
1 cup shredded sharp cheddar cheese
4 green onions, including green tops, thinly sliced

DIRECTIONS

Preheat broiler to high.

In a large skillet over medium heat, melt butter. Cook gnocchi in a single layer until golden brown and toasted on all sides, about 3 minutes per side. Remove from skillet and set aside.

Return skillet to medium heat. Brown ground beef, stirring to crumble, until thoroughly cooked and no longer pink. Drain excess grease. Add salt and pepper, cumin, paprika, mustard powder, onion and garlic. Cook about 5 minutes or until onion is tender, stirring occasionally.

Add tomatoes, broth and gnocchi to the skillet. Stir. Bring to a boil, reduce to a simmer, and cover. Simmer for about 5 minutes or until gnocchi is tender and the liquid is mostly reduced. Remove from the heat.

Add cream and ½ the cheese and stir well. Top with remaining cheese. Broil for about 4 minutes until cheese is melted and bubbly. Top with scallions and serve.

One Pot Cheeseburger Casserole

INGREDIENTS

1 ½ pounds ground beef

1 onion, diced

2 teaspoons kosher salt

1 teaspoon freshly cracked black pepper

1 28-ounce can diced tomatoes, with juices

1 8-ounce can tomato sauce

2 cups chicken broth

¼ cup ketchup

1 tablespoon Dijon mustard

1 16-ounce package rotini

2 cups water

2 cups shredded cheddar cheese

1 Roma tomato, diced

4 green onions, including green tops, thinly sliced

DIRECTIONS

In a Dutch oven over medium heat, cook ground beef until brown, stirring occasionally to crumble, until cooked through and no longer pink. Drain excess grease. Add onion, season with salt and pepper and cook an additional 5 minutes or until onion is tender.

Stir in tomatoes, tomato sauce, chicken broth, ketchup, mustard, pasta and water. Bring to a boil, reduce to a simmer, and simmer about 15 minutes, or until pasta is tender. Remove from heat and top with cheese. Replace cover and allow to sit until cheese has melted, about 5 minutes. Sprinkle with tomato and green onion and serve.

Italian Wedding Soup

INGREDIENTS

For the meatballs

1 onion, grated
1/3 cup fresh parsley, chopped
1 large egg
2 garlic cloves, minced
2 teaspoons kosher salt
1 teaspoon freshly cracked black pepper
1 slice white or wheat bread, crusts removed, grated or crumbled
½ cup Parmesan cheese, Parmesan
1-pound ground beef

For the soup

12 cups chicken broth
1 box frozen chopped spinach, defrosted and squeezed
8-ounces Acini de Pepe or another tiny pasta
2 tablespoons Parmesan cheese

DIRECTIONS

In a large bowl, combine onion, parsley, egg, garlic, salt, pepper and bread crumbs. Mix well. Add ground beef and Parmesan cheese and mix thoroughly. Shape mixture into ½ inch meatballs and place on a baking sheet.

In a large <u>saucepan</u>, bring broth and spinach to a boil. Add uncooked meatballs and bring back to a boil. Reduce to a simmer, and simmer for 5 minutes, stirring gently on occasion to prevent sticking. Add pasta and continue to simmer until pasta is tender and meatballs are cooked through. Taste and adjust for seasoning. Sprinkle with Parmesan cheese and serve.

Stuffed French Bread Sandwiches

INGREDIENTS

1 loaf French bread
1-pound ground beef
¼ cup finely chopped onion
¼ cup finely chopped celery
2 cloves garlic, minced
1 ¼ cups cream of mushroom soup (1 can)
2 tablespoons milk
2 teaspoons Worcestershire sauce
2 teaspoons kosher salt
1 teaspoon freshly cracked black pepper
1 ½ cups shredded cheddar cheese
1 tablespoon fresh parsley, chopped

DIRECTIONS

Preheat oven to 350F.

Slice French loaf in half, lengthwise. Scoop the bread out of the center of each half to create pockets, and place into a large bowl. Tear into small pieces and set aside. Place French loaf halves on a baking sheet and set aside.

In a large skillet over medium heat, brown ground beef, stirring to crumble, until cooked through and no longer pink. Drain excess grease. Add onion, celery and garlic to the skillet and cook for about 5 minutes or until vegetables are fragrant and tender.

Stir in soup, milk, Worcestershire sauce, salt and pepper. Bring to a boil, reduce to a bare simmer, and simmer for about 5 minutes. Remove from heat. Stir in bread crumbs.

Spoon mixture into one of the French bread shells. Top with the shredded cheddar cheese and top with the second bread shell.

Bake for 15 minutes, or until cheese is melted and bubbly. Allow to rest for at least 5 minutes, then slice to serve.

5-Ingredient Chili

INGREDIENTS

1-pound ground beef

3 15-ounce cans diced tomatoes with green chilies

2 15-ounce cans beans – your choice, black beans, kidney beans, pinto beans or a combination

1 onion, diced

2 tablespoons chili powder

Toppings of your choice: diced tomato, thinly sliced green onion, sour cream, minced cilantro, shredded cheddar, salsa, tortilla chips, etc.

DIRECTIONS

In a Dutch oven, brown ground beef over medium heat, stirring to crumble, until cooked through and no longer pink. Drain excess grease, and stir in remaining ingredients. Bring to a boil, reduce to a simmer, and simmer 15 minutes. Serve with your choice of toppings.

Cheeseburger Egg Rolls

INGREDIENTS

For the egg rolls:

1-pound ground beef
½ onion, minced
1 teaspoon kosher salt
1 teaspoon freshly cracked black pepper
5 slices cheese, broken into small pieces
½ cup diced dill pickles
14 egg roll wrappers
1 egg white
Oil for frying

For the sauce:

¼ cup mayonnaise
1 tablespoon tomato paste
1 clove garlic, minced
1 teaspoon paprika
Kosher salt and freshly cracked black pepper, to taste

DIRECTIONS

In a large skillet over medium heat, brown ground beef, stirring to crumble, until cooked through and no longer pink. Pour off excess grease. Add onion, salt and pepper and cook until onion is tender, about 5 minutes.

Remove from heat. Stir in cheese and pickles and allow to sit for a few minutes for cheese to melt.

Heat oil to 350F.

In a small bowl, whisk egg whites.

To roll the eggs rolls, place an egg roll on the counter, point toward you. Place about 2 tablespoons of the meat mixture in the center, leaving an inch on all sides. Fold the corner of the wrapper closest to you over the filling, tucking the edge under. Fold both sides toward the center of the wrapper. With a small brush or your fingertip, brush egg white on edges of the wrapper, and roll the egg roll over to seal. Place seam side down on a baking sheet while the oil heats and you roll the remainder of the egg rolls.

Fry egg rolls in batches, until golden brown and crispy, about 5 minutes, turning as necessary to fry each side. Drain on paper towels.

Whisk all sauce ingredients in a medium bowl, and serve with hot egg rolls.

Enchilada Zucchini Boats

INGREDIENTS

1-pound ground beef
1 onion, diced
3 garlic cloves, minced
1 teaspoon smoked paprika
1 teaspoon ground cumin
2 teaspoons kosher salt
3 large zucchinis
1½ cups red enchilada sauce
½ cup shredded cheddar cheese
¼ cup chopped fresh cilantro
Toppings: diced tomatoes, diced green onions, diced avocado, salsa, tortilla chips

DIRECTIONS

Preheat oven to 350F. Lightly grease a 9x13 baking dish.

Slice the zucchinis in half lengthwise. Scoop out enough of the flesh to make a 'boat', leaving just enough flesh on the walls of the boat to make sure they don't collapse. Put in casserole dish and set aside.

In a large skillet over medium heat, brown the ground beef, stirring to crumble, until cooked through and no longer pink. Drain excess grease. Add onion to the skillet, and cook until onions are tender, about 5 minutes.

Add garlic, paprika, cumin, salt and pepper, Stir well and remove from heat.

Spoon beef mixture into the zucchini boats. Pour enchilada sauce over the meat mixture and sprinkle with the cheddar cheese. Cover with foil. Bake in preheated oven for 20 minutes.

Remove foil, return dish to the oven and bake an additional 5 minutes. Sprinkle with cilantro and serve with tomatoes, avocados, salsa, green onions and tortilla chips.

Tamale Pie

INGREDIENTS

For the cornbread:

½ cup cornmeal
2/3 cup flour
3 tablespoons sugar
1 tablespoon baking powder
1 teaspoon kosher salt
4 tablespoons olive oil
1/3 cup milk
1 egg
1 4.5-ounce can green chilies
1 can corn

For the filling:

1-pound ground beef
2 teaspoons cumin
2 teaspoons chili powder
2 teaspoons kosher salt
1 teaspoon freshly cracked black pepper
1 ¼ cup enchilada sauce
2 cups shredded cheddar cheese
Toppings: salsa, guacamole, sour cream, shredded cheddar, fresh cilantro, limes

DIRECTIONS

Preheat oven to 400F. Lightly grease a 9x13 baking dish, or a large cast iron skillet.

In a large mixing bowl, whisk together cornmeal, flour, sugar, baking powder and salt. Stir in oil until soft crumbles form. Whisk in milk and eggs. Fold in green chiles and corn. Pour into prepared baking dish and bake until set, about 25 minutes.

Meanwhile, in a large skillet over medium heat, cook ground beef, stirring to crumble, until cooked through and no longer pink. Drain excess grease. Add cumin, chili powder, salt and pepper. Stir well.

When cornbread has baked, reduce oven to 350F. Poke holes all over the top of the cornbread with a fork. Pour enchilada sauce over the top of the cornbread, and top with the ground beef and then the cheese. Cover with foil.

Bake for 20 minutes, and remove foil. Bake an additional 10 minutes and allow tamale pie to cool for 15 minutes before serving. Serve with additional toppings, salsa, sour cream, cheese, cilantro and limes.

Beef and Barley Soup

INGREDIENTS

1 ½ pounds ground beef
6 cups beef broth
2 carrots, peeled and diced
1 onion, diced
1 green pepper, diced
2 stalks celery, diced
3-4 cloves garlic, minced
½ cup barley
2 teaspoons kosher salt
1 teaspoon freshly cracked black pepper
2 bay leaves
1/3 cup ketchup
1 38-ounce can crushed tomatoes, undrained
1 8-ounce can tomato sauce

DIRECTIONS

In a Dutch oven over medium heat, brown ground beef, stirring to crumble, until fully cooked and no longer pink. Drain excess grease.

Place all remaining ingredients into the Dutch oven. Bring to a boil, reduce to a simmer. Simmer for just at 1 ½ hours. Taste and adjust for seasoning and serve.

Cheeseburger Soup

INGREDIENTS

3 russet potatoes, peeled and diced

1 onion, diced

2 carrots, shredded

1 stalk celery, diced

2 teaspoons dried basil

2 teaspoons dried parsley

3 cups chicken broth

1-pound ground beef

3 tablespoons butter

¼ cup flour

2 cups milk

2 teaspoons kosher salt

1 teaspoon freshly cracked black pepper

2 cups shredded cheddar cheese

DIRECTIONS

In a large Dutch oven, brown ground beef, stirring to crumble, until fully cooked and no longer pink. Drain excess grease. Place potatoes, onions, carrots, celery, basil and parsley in the Dutch oven. Cook until vegetables are tender, about 7-10 minutes.

Add butter, and sprinkle vegetables with the flour. Stir well. Whisk in chicken broth and milk. Bring to a boil, reduce to a simmer, and simmer for about 15 minutes. Sprinkle in shredded cheese, and stir well, until cheese is fully melted. Serve hot.

Hashweh, Ground Beef and Rice with Nuts

INGREDIENTS

1 ½ cups rice
2 tablespoons olive oil, divided
1 red onion, diced
1 pound very lean ground beef
1 ¾ teaspoons allspice
2 teaspoons garlic powder
¾ teaspoons ground cloves
¾ teaspoons cinnamon
2 teaspoons kosher salt
1 teaspoon freshly ground black pepper
½ cup fresh parsley leaves, chopped
½ cup pine nuts, toasted
½ cup slivered almonds, toasted
½ cup raisins

DIRECTIONS

Soak rice in cold water for about 15-20 minutes. Drain well.

Meanwhile, in a Dutch oven, heat olive oil. Sauté red onion for about 5 minutes. Add ground beef, stirring to crumble. Season with allspice, cloves, and cinnamon.

Add salt and pepper, and stirring occasionally, cook until fully cooked.

Add rice to the pot. Add water and remaining olive oil. Bring to a boil and reduce to a simmer. Simmer uncovered until liquid has reduced by half.

Cover and continue to simmer until liquid is fully absorbed. Remove from heat.

Place a large serving platter upside down over pot. Carefully flip the pot so that the contents hit the platter, and the meat layer now tops the rice.

Garnish with parsley, toasted pine nuts, almonds and raisins.

Kofta Kebabs with Tzatziki

INGREDIENTS

For the kebabs

4 cloves garlic
1 pinch kosher salt
1 tablespoon kosher salt
1-pound ground beef
3 tablespoons grated onion
3 tablespoons fresh parsley, chopped
1 tablespoon coriander
1 teaspoon cumin
½ teaspoon allspice
¼ teaspoon cayenne
¼ teaspoon ground ginger
1 teaspoon freshly cracked black pepper

For the tzatziki

2 cups plain Greek yogurt
1 cucumber, peeled, halved, and seeded
2 teaspoons kosher salt
Pinch of kosher salt
2 cloves garlic
2 teaspoons lemon juice
1 tablespoon olive oil
½ teaspoon dried mint
Flat bread, toasted or grilled

DIRECTIONS

Make the tzatziki sauce: grate the cucumber into a medium bowl. Sprinkle with kosher salt, mix well and set aside to rest for about 20 minutes. Squeeze as much liquid as possible from the cucumber.

Place the garlic cloves on a cutting board. Sprinkle with a pinch of kosher salt. With the back of a spoon or the flat of a knife, mash garlic and salt to form a rough paste. Stir in the cucumber, olive oil, lemon juice, mint and yogurt. Stir well and chill at least 1 hour before serving.

Make the kebabs: Place the garlic cloves on a cutting board. Sprinkle with a pinch of kosher salt. With the back of a spoon or the flat of a knife, mash garlic and salt to form a rough paste.

In a large mixing bowl, combine garlic paste with ground beef, kosher salt, onion, parsley, coriander, cumin, allspice, cayenne, ginger and black pepper.

Line a baking sheet with foil. Divide the meat mixture into 28 equal pieces. Mold each piece around the end of a skewer, making an oval shaped patty around the skewer, about 2 inches in size and covering the pointed end of the skewer. Place on the baking sheet as you complete them. Cover and chill for at least 30 minutes and up to overnight.

Heat a grill or heat a grill pan over medium heat. Lightly oil grill or pan, and working a few at a time, cook the kebabs, turning to brown evenly on all sides, about 5-6 minutes. Transfer to a serving platter and serve with flat bread and tzatziki sauce.

Stuffed Eggplant

INGREDIENTS

2 eggplants
1 tablespoon olive oil
½ cup pine nuts, toasted
1-pound ground beef
1 ½ teaspoons cinnamon
¼ teaspoon nutmeg
¼ teaspoon nutmeg
¼ teaspoon allspice
2 teaspoons kosher salt
1 teaspoon freshly cracked pepper
1 large onion, diced
½ cup chicken broth
1 32-ounce can crushed tomatoes

DIRECTIONS

Preheat broiler. Line a baking sheet with foil.

Cut the eggplants into 2 inch rounds and place on the baking sheet. Brush eggplant on both sides with olive oil and season with salt and pepper. Broil for about 5 minutes per side, until golden brown.

Transfer eggplant to a 9x13 casserole dish. Reduce oven to 350F.

In a large skillet over medium heat, brown ground beef, stirring to crumble, until cooked through and no longer pink. <u>Drain</u> excess grease. Season with salt and pepper, cinnamon, nutmeg and allspice. Add onions and cook, stirring occasionally, about 5 minutes or until onions are tender.

Add chicken broth and stir to deglaze, scraping up the brown bits. Stir in tomatoes and pine nuts, and remove from heat. Pour meat mixture over the eggplant. Bake for 45 minutes, until hot and bubbly. Serve with yogurt, parsley and pine nuts.

Kheema, Indian Ground Beef with Peas

INGREDIENTS

3 tablespoons olive oil

1 onion, finely diced

4 cloves garlic, minced

1 (1-inch piece) fresh ginger, peeled and grated

2 teaspoons coriander

1 teaspoon paprika

1 teaspoon garam masala

1 teaspoon ground cumin

½ teaspoon cayenne, optional

1-pound ground beef

2 tomatoes, chopped

1 cup water

2 teaspoons kosher salt

1 teaspoon freshly cracked black pepper

Kosher salt and freshly ground black pepper

½ cup fresh or frozen peas

2 teaspoons apple cider vinegar

¼ cup chopped fresh cilantro

4 pitas, warmed

DIRECTIONS

In a large skillet over medium heat, cook ground beef until browned, stirring to crumble, about 5 minutes. Drain excess grease. Set beef aside.

In the same skillet, heat olive oil over medium heat. Add the onions and sauté about 5 minutes, until onions are tender. Add garlic and ginger and sauté another 30 seconds or so. Stir in coriander, paprika, garam masala, cumin and cayenne, and cook 2 minutes. Return beef to skillet.

Add tomatoes, water, salt and pepper. Stir in peas. Bring to a boil, reduce to a simmer, and simmer about 10 minutes. Stir in vinegar and cilantro. Serve with warm pita bread.

Spicy Indian Style Meatballs

INGREDIENTS

1-pound lean ground beef
2 tablespoons olive oil
1 onion, minced
1 tablespoon garlic paste
1 teaspoon ginger paste
1 ½ teaspoon cayenne pepper
¼ teaspoon red pepper flakes
2 teaspoons garam masala
½ cup cilantro, minced
Salt to taste

DIRECTIONS

Preheat oven to 400F. Line a baking sheet with parchment or foil. Set aside.

In a large bowl, mix together all ingredients except for the ground beef. Add beef and mix just until combined, being careful not to overmix. Form into 1 inch meatballs and place on prepared baking sheet.

Bake for about 45 minutes or until golden brown all over, turning the meatballs halfway through. Allow meatballs to rest 5-10 minutes before serving.

Moussaka

INGREDIENTS

3 eggplants, peeled and sliced into ½ inch thick slices
2 teaspoons kosher salt
3 tablespoons olive oil
1-pound ground beef
2 teaspoons kosher salt
1 teaspoon freshly cracked black pepper
2 onions, diced
2 cloves garlic, minced
¼ teaspoon cinnamon
¼ teaspoon nutmeg, freshly grated
1 teaspoon fines herbs
¼ cup fresh parsley, minced
1 8-ounce can tomato paste
½ cup red wine
1 egg, lightly beaten
½ cup butter
6 tablespoons flour
4 cups milk
1 teaspoon kosher salt
1 teaspoon freshly cracked black pepper
1 ½ cup parmesan cheese
¼ teaspoon nutmeg, freshly grated

DIRECTIONS

Sprinkle eggplant slices with salt. Set on paper towels, and let them sit for ½ hour to draw out excess moisture.

Place a skillet over medium high heat. Heat oil, and fry eggplant on both sides until browned. Drain on paper towels and sets aside.

In the same skillet, brown ground beef, stirring to crumble, until fully cooked and no longer pink. Drain excess grease. Add salt, pepper, onions, garlic, cinnamon, nutmeg, fines herbs and parsley. Cook for about five minutes, stirring occasionally, until onions are tender.

Add tomato sauce and wine. Stir well. Bring to a boil, reduce to a simmer and simmer for 20 minutes. Allow to cool, then stir in egg. Preheat oven to 350F, and lightly grease a 9x13 casserole dish.

Meanwhile, make the béchamel sauce. In a large skillet over medium heat, melt butter. Whisk in flour, and cook for about 1 minute. Slowly whisk in milk, and season with salt and pepper.

Arrange eggplant in a single layer in the bottom of the baking dish. Top with the meat sauce, and sprinkle ½ the parmesan over the sauce. Cover with another layer of eggplant, and another ½ cup cheese. Pour béchamel sauce over the top layer of eggplant, and top with remaining cheese.

Bake for 1 hour. Allow to rest for at least 10 minutes before serving.

Arrange a layer of eggplant in a greased 9x13 inch baking dish. Cover eggplant with all of the meat mixture, and then sprinkle 1/2 cup of Parmesan cheese over the meat. Cover with remaining eggplant, and sprinkle another 1/2 cup of cheese on top. Pour the béchamel sauce over the top, and sprinkle with the nutmeg. Sprinkle with the remaining cheese.

Greek Bifteki

INGREDIENTS

1 1/3-pounds ground beef
1 tablespoon plain yogurt
2 teaspoons dried thyme
2 teaspoons kosher salt
1 teaspoon freshly cracked black pepper
4-ounces feta cheese, sliced

DIRECTIONS

In a large bowl, mix together beef, yogurt, thyme, salt and pepper. Shape meat into 8 patties.

Place a slice of cheese onto each of 4 patties. Top with a second patty, and press to seal the edges around the cheese.

In a large skillet, cook patties about 7 minutes per side, until cooked through and cheese is melted. You can also use a grill plate or broiler.

Greek Souzoukaklia

INGREDIENTS

1 ½-pounds ground beef
1 onion, diced
1/3 cup raisins, chopped
2 teaspoons parsley, chopped
½ teaspoon cayenne pepper
½ teaspoon cinnamon
½ teaspoon coriander
1/8 teaspoon nutmeg
2 teaspoons kosher salt
1 teaspoon freshly cracked black pepper
1 tablespoon olive oil

DIRECTIONS

In a large bowl, mix together all ingredients. Shape mixture into 6 patties, and fold patties around skewers.

Grill skewers, or cook in a medium hot pan for approximately 10-12 minutes, turning to brown all over, until cooked through.

Pastitsio

INGREDIENTS

8-ounces macaroni
1 egg, lightly beaten
¼ cup Parmesan
4-5 Roma tomatoes, small dice
1-pound ground beef
½ onion, diced
2 cloves garlic, minced
8-ounces tomato sauce
¼ cup chicken stock
1 tablespoon red wine vinegar
1 tablespoon chili powder
½ teaspoon ground allspice
¼ teaspoon cinnamon
3 tablespoons butter
3 tablespoon flour
2 teaspoons kosher salt
1 teaspoon black pepper
1 ½ cups milk
1 egg, lightly beaten
¼ cup Parmesan cheese

DIRECTIONS

Preheat oven to 350F.

In a large pot of lightly salted boiling water, cook macaroni according to package direction. Drain. Stir in egg and ¼ cup Parmesan. Set aside.

In a large skillet over medium heat, brown ground beef, stirring occasionally, until cooked through. Drain off excess grease. Stir in onions and garlic and cook for about 5 minutes, until onion is fragrant and tender.

Stir in tomatoes, sauce, chicken broth, vinegar, chili powder, allspice, cinnamon and salt. Bring to a boil, reduce to a simmer, and simmer for about 20 minutes, or until thickened.

Meanwhile, melt butter in a saucepan. Whisk in flour, salt and pepper, and cook for 1 minute. Slowly whisk in milk, and cook, whisking constantly, until smooth, thickened and bubbly. Pour ¼ of the white sauce into a separate bowl and whisk in egg. Return egg mixture to the pot with remaining white sauce. Stir in ¼ cup parmesan cheese.

Place ½ the pasta in the bottom of a 9x13 casserole dish. Add meat sauce, then remaining pasta. Pour white sauce over the pasta layer.

Bake for 30-40 minutes until bubbly throughout. Let casserole rest for at least 5 minutes before serving.

Keftedes (Greek Meatballs)

INGREDIENTS

4 slices bread, torn into pieces
2 tablespoons milk
2 cloves garlic, minced
1 onion, finely minced
4 teaspoons dried mint
2 teaspoons kosher salt
1 teaspoon freshly cracked black pepper
1-pound ground beef
4 eggs
1 cup flour
vegetable oil for frying

DIRECTIONS

In a small bowl, mix together bread and milk. Set aside.

In a large bowl, stir together garlic, onion, mint, salt and pepper. Stir in bread/milk mixture. Add ground beef and mix just until combined.

Shape into 1-2 inch meatballs. Place flour in a shallow dish, and add meatballs. Toss meatballs in the flour to coat. Transfer meatballs to a baking sheet, shaking off excess flour.

Heat 1-inch oil to 350F. Add meatballs, a few at a time, and cook until cooked through and no pink appears, about 10 minutes. Drain on paper towels.

Greek Lasagna

INGREDIENTS

16-ounces macaroni
2-pounds ground beef
1 onion, diced
1 cup Parmesan cheese
4-ounces feta cheese
1 15-ounce can diced tomatoes
1 teaspoon cinnamon
2 teaspoons kosher salt
1 teaspoon freshly cracked black pepper
3 cups milk
3 tablespoons cornstarch
¼ cup butter

DIRECTIONS

Preheat oven to 350F.

In a large pot of lightly salted water, cook macaroni according to package directions. Drain and set aside.

Meanwhile, in a large skillet over medium heat, cook ground beef, stirring to crumble, until cooked through and no longer pink. Drain excess grease. Add onion and cook for about 5 minutes, or until onion is tender and fragrant. Stir in tomatoes, feta, Parmesan, cinnamon, salt and pepper. Transfer to a 9x13 baking dish.

In a saucepan over medium heat, mix together the milk and cornstarch until no lumps remain. Add butter, and bring to a boil. Boil for 1 minute, then remove from heat, and pour the sauce over the mixture in the baking dish.

Bake for 1 hour, until the top is golden brown. Let stand for 10 minutes before serving.

Yemistes – Greek Style Stuffed Tomatoes

INGREDIENTS

10 large tomatoes
1 ½ pounds ground beef
¼ cups olive oil
¼ cup olive oil
1 onion, finely diced
½ cup rice
¼ cup fresh parsley
2 teaspoons kosher salt
1 teaspoon freshly cracked black pepper
¼ teaspoon cinnamon

DIRECTIONS

Carefully slice a piece from the top of each tomato, and remove the pulp with a teaspoon, leaving a wall for support. Set pulp aside.

Arrange tomatoes in a large casserole dish and set aside.

In a large skillet over medium heat, cook ground beef, stirring to crumble, until cooked through. Drain excess grease. Add olive oil and onion to the beef and cook for about 5 minutes, or until onion is tender and fragrant.

Add rice, parsley, salt, pepper, cinnamon, and 1 cup of the reserved tomato pulp. Bring to a boil, reduce to a bare simmer, and simmer for about 10 minutes on low. Remove from heat and allow to cool.

Fill tomato shells with the meat mixture, leaving a little room for the rice to swell. Replace the tops, Drizzle the tomatoes with olive oil. Add about 1 cup of the reserved tomato pulp to the bottom of the baking dish.

Bake for about 1 hour and 15 minutes, and allow to rest for at least 5 minutes before serving.

Youverlakia - Greek Meatball Soup with Egg Lemon Sauce

For the soup:

1-pound ground beef
1 onion, grated
2 teaspoons kosher salt
1 teaspoon freshly cracked black pepper
2 teaspoons parsley, chopped
½ cup rice, uncooked
1 egg, lightly beaten
2 tablespoons flour
4 cups chicken broth
1 cup tomato juice
¼ cup butter
2 teaspoons kosher salt
1 teaspoon freshly cracked black pepper

Lemon Sauce:

3 eggs
2 tablespoons water
1 lemon

DIRECTIONS

In a medium mixing bowl, combine ground beef, onion, salt, pepper, parsley, half the rice and egg. Form into small bite-sized meatballs. Dust meatballs with flour.

In a Dutch oven or stockpot bring broth, tomato juice, butter, salt and pepper to a boil. Add remaining rice and carefully drop in meatballs. Reduce heat to a simmer, cover and simmer for about 30 minutes. Turn off heat.

In a small bowl whisk eggs with 2 tablespoons water. Carefully add about ½ cup of the soup to the eggs, stirring constantly. Whisk in lemon juice. Slowly pour egg mixture over the meatballs, stirring to combine. Serve immediately.

SAUCES AND SEASONINGS

Ricky's Salsa

My son Ricky - who is my budding chef (he's 12!) - came up with this fresh salsa. I love it. Can't be better.

INGREDIENTS

6-7 Roma or small tomatoes, seeded and diced
1 small bell pepper, seeded and diced
1 bunch green onions, tops included, minced
2-3 cloves garlic, minced
2 limes - juiced
1 chipotle chili, (canned) plus about 1 tablespoon of reserved sauce
1 tablespoon minced parsley
1 tablespoon minced cilantro
1 teaspoon kosher salt

DIRECTIONS

Mix all ingredients in the bowl of a food processor, and pulse 3-4 times until well combined, but still chunky. Adjust salt to taste.

Italian Seasoning

INGREDIENTS

2 tablespoons dried basil

2 tablespoons dried oregano

2 tablespoons dried rosemary

2 tablespoons dried marjoram

2 tablespoons dried thyme

2 tablespoons dried savory

2 tablespoons red pepper flakes

DIRECTIONS

Combine all ingredients in a bowl and whisk together to blend well, or pulse in the bowl of a food processor for a finer consistency. Cover tightly and store in a cool, dark place.

Chili Powder

INGREDIENTS

2 tablespoons paprika

2 teaspoons oregano

1 ½ teaspoons cumin

1 ½ teaspoons garlic powder

¾ teaspoon onion powder

½ teaspoon cayenne pepper, or to taste (optional)

DIRECTIONS

Combine all ingredients in a bowl and whisk together to blend well, or pulse in the bowl of a food processor for a finer consistency. Cover tightly and store in a cool, dark place.

Greek Seasoning Blend

INGREDIENTS

2 teaspoons salt

2 teaspoons garlic powder

2 teaspoons dried basil

2 teaspoons dried oregano

1 teaspoon ground cinnamon

1 teaspoon ground black pepper

1 teaspoon dried parsley

1 teaspoon dried rosemary, minced

1 teaspoon dried dill weed

1 teaspoon dried marjoram

½ teaspoon ground thyme

½ teaspoon ground nutmeg

DIRECTIONS

Combine all ingredients in a bowl and whisk together to blend well, or pulse in the bowl of a food processor for a finer consistency. Cover tightly and store in a cool, dark place.

Taco Seasoning

INGREDIENTS

1 tablespoon chili powder

¼ teaspoon garlic powder

¼ teaspoon onion powder

¼ teaspoon crushed red pepper flakes

¼ teaspoon dried oregano

½ teaspoon paprika

1 ½ teaspoons ground cumin

1 teaspoon kosher salt

1 teaspoon black pepper

DIRECTIONS

Combine all ingredients in a bowl and whisk together to blend well, or pulse in the bowl of a food processor for a finer consistency. Cover tightly and store in a cool, dark place.

Curry Powder

INGREDIENTS

2 tablespoons ground cumin
2 tablespoons ground coriander
2 teaspoons ground turmeric
½ teaspoon crushed red pepper flakes
½ teaspoon mustard seed
½ teaspoon ground ginger

DIRECTIONS

Combine all ingredients in a bowl and whisk together to blend well, or pulse in the bowl of a food processor for a finer consistency. Cover tightly and store in a cool, dark place.

Chipotle Salsa

INGREDIENTS

2-pounds tomatoes

2 unpeeled white onions, cut in half horizontally

20 unpeeled garlic cloves

15 dried chipotle chilies (3 oz. total) or 10 canned chipotles

3 tablespoons olive oil

½ cup lime juice

2 teaspoons kosher salt

DIRECTIONS

Cover a large grill pan or heavy skillet with foil and set over medium high heat. Once hot, add tomatoes, onions and garlic. Turn occasionally to develop brown spots all over the ingredients. As they brown, remove each item and set aside.

Add dried chilies (if using) and turn until just softened, a minute or two. Set aside.

Using gloves, stem chilies and remove seeds. Break into pieces and drop into blender or food processor. Core tomatoes and cut into chunks. Add to the blender or food processor. Peel onions and garlic, and roughly chop onions, and add both to the blender or food processor. Process until smooth.

Over medium high heat, add olive oil to a large skillet. Add tomato mixture, lime juice and salt. Bring to a simmer and stirring occasionally, simmer for about 15 minutes, or until thickened.

Montreal Steak Seasoning

INGREDIENTS

2 tablespoons paprika

2 tablespoons black pepper

2 tablespoons kosher salt

1 tablespoon garlic powder

1 tablespoon onion powder

1 tablespoon coriander

1 tablespoon dill

1 tablespoon crushed red pepper flakes

DIRECTIONS

Combine all ingredients in a bowl and whisk together to blend well. Cover tightly and store in a cool, dark place.

Cajun Spice Mix

INGREDIENTS

2 teaspoons salt

2 teaspoons garlic powder

2 ½ teaspoons paprika

1 teaspoon ground black pepper

1 teaspoon onion powder

 1 teaspoon cayenne pepper

1 ¼ teaspoons dried oregano

1 ¼ teaspoons dried thyme

½ teaspoon red pepper flakes (optional)

DIRECTIONS

Combine all ingredients in a bowl and whisk together to blend well. Cover tightly and store in a cool, dark place.

Homemade Marinara Sauce Recipe

INGREDIENTS

½ cup extra-virgin olive oil

1 large onion, finely chopped

4 garlic cloves, crushed

2 stalks celery, finely chopped

1 teaspoon kosher salt (or to taste)

½ teaspoon freshly ground pepper (to taste)

2 (32-oz) cans crushed tomatoes

2 dried bay leaves

A pinch of red pepper flakes (optional)

2 tablespoons dried oregano

DIRECTIONS

In a large pot over medium high heat, heat olive oil. Add onions, garlic and celery and sauté until onions are translucent and fragrant, about 10 minutes.

Add tomatoes, salt, pepper, red pepper flakes, bay leaves and oregano. Bring to a boil, reduce to a bare simmer and simmer for about 1 hour, until sauce thickens.

Remove bay leaf. Taste, and adjust for salt and pepper.

Enchilada Sauce

INGREDIENTS

6 dried ancho chilies
Boiling water
1 6-ounce can tomato paste
¼ cup corn oil
2 cloves garlic, minced
2 teaspoons kosher salt
1 teaspoon dried oregano
¼ teaspoon ground cumin
3 cups beef broth

DIRECTIONS

Preheat oven to 400F.

Place chilies on a baking sheet. Toast chilies for about 5 minutes. Remove stems, ribs and seeds and place chilies in a bowl. Cover with enough hot water to completely submerge and set aside to soak for about an hour.

In the bowl of a food processor combine chilies, tomato paste, oil, garlic, salt, oregano, cumin and 1 cup of the beef broth. Process until smooth. Transfer to a saucepan, add remaining beef broth and bring to a boil. Reduce heat to a simmer, and simmer for 10 minutes.

STOCKS AND PASTRIES

Corn Muffin Mix

INGREDIENTS

2/3 cup all-purpose flour
½ cup yellow cornmeal
3 tablespoons sugar
1 tablespoon baking powder
¼ teaspoon salt
2 tablespoons vegetable oil
To make muffins add:
1 egg
1/3 cup milk

DIRECTIONS

In a medium bowl, combine flour, cornmeal, sugar, baking powder and salt.

Whisk in oil and whisk until mixture is dry and smooth.

If your recipe calls for a box of cornbread mix, add the mixture to that recipe.

If you wish to make corn muffins, preheat oven to 400F. Lightly grease a muffin pan. Stir egg and milk into dry mixture. Fill muffin pan ½ full, and bake for 20 minutes or until golden brown.

Homemade Ranch Dressing Seasoning Mix

INGREDIENTS

2 tablespoons dried parsley
1 teaspoon dried dill
1 teaspoon garlic powder
1 teaspoon onion powder
½ teaspoon dried basil
½ teaspoon pepper

DIRECTIONS

Add all ingredients to a small bowl and mix well.

To make dressing, whisk together 1/3 cup mayonnaise and ¼ cup milk or buttermilk, whichever you prefer. Add 1 tablespoon of the seasoning mix, stir well. Taste for seasoning, and add kosher salt to taste.

Homemade Italian Breaderumbs

INGREDIENTS

4 slices stale bread
1 tablespoon Italian seasoning
1 teaspoon garlic powder
½ teaspoon kosher salt

DIRECTIONS

Preheat oven to 300F.

Place all ingredients into the bowl of a food processor. Pulse until bread has formed ccarse crumbs. Spread onto a baking sheet.

Toast crumbs about 5 minutes, stirring occasionally, until brown and crispy.

Pie Crust

For 1 9-inch pie

INGREDIENTS

1 ¾ cups flour
2 teaspoons sugar
1 teaspoon kosher salt
6 tablespoons cold butter, cut into small pieces
¼ cup cold shortening
6-8 tablespoons ice water

DIRECTIONS

In a large mixing bowl, combine flour, sugar and salt. Add butter and shortening and toss to coat.

With your fingers, rub the butter to incorporate the flour, until butter is about the size of peas. Slowly drizzle in ice water adding only just enough to allow the dough to come together. Shape into a ball, cover and chill for ½ hour.

Lightly sprinkle work surface with flour. Press the ball of dough to flatten it. With a rolling pin shape dough into a 9-inch circle and transfer to a pie plate.

Celery Salt

INGREDIENTS

Leaves from one bunch of celery
Kosher salt

DIRECTIONS

Preheat oven to 350F. Place celery leaves in a single layer on a baking sheet. Toast leaves for about 5-7 minutes, just until dehydrated and crispy, but not browned.

Place dry leaves into the bowl of a food processor, and add an equal amount of kosher salt. Process until leaves are crumbled.

Rotel Copycat Recipe

INGREDIENTS

4-pounds tomatoes, chopped and seeded
12 jalapeno peppers
2 teaspoons kosher salt

DIRECTIONS

Place all ingredients into a saucepan, and bring to a boil over medium heat. Reduce to a simmer, and simmer until reduced to 1 quart.

Chicken Broth

INGREDIENTS

1 whole chicken, about 4-5 pounds
1 onion, peeled and quartered
2 carrots, roughly chopped
2 stalks celery, roughly chopped
4-5 sprigs fresh thyme
4-5 sprigs fresh parsley
1 teaspoon whole peppercorns
1 bay leaf
Enough water to cover

DIRECTIONS

Place all ingredients into a Dutch oven or large stockpot. Add enough water to cover. Bring to a boil, reduce to a bare simmer, and simmer for about an hour.

While the broth simmers, use a spoon or a ladle to skim off any fat and scum that rises to the surface. Remove chicken from the pot and allow to cool for about 10 minutes. Pull meat from the bones, and return bones to the pot. Allow to simmer about another hour.

Pour broth through a strainer, and chill until ready to use. Any remaining fat will solidify at the top of the broth and can be lifted off with a spoon.

Beef Stock

INGREDIENTS

6-7pounds beef bones
1 onion, quartered
3 carrots, roughly chopped
½ cup water
2 stalks celery, roughly chopped
1 large tomato
1 teaspoon whole peppercorns
4 sprigs fresh parsley
4 sprigs fresh thyme
1 bay leaf
1 tablespoon salt
4 cloves garlic
12 cups water or enough to cover

DIRECTIONS

Preheat oven to 450F. Place bones, onion and carrot into a roasting pan, and roast for about 30 minutes, turning ingredients occasionally to brown well.

Place bones, onion and carrot into a large stockpot or Dutch oven. Drain excess fat from the roasting pan, and pour in ½ cup of water. Scrape any brown bits from bottom of roasting pan, and pour this into the stockpot.

Add remaining ingredients to the pot. Bring to a boil, reduce to a simmer, and simmer for about 4 hours, skimming off any fat or scum that rises to the top.

Pour stock through a strainer and chill until ready to use.

Condensed Cream of Mushroom Soup Substitute

INGREDIENTS

1 tablespoon butter
2 tablespoons flour
½ cup chicken or beef broth
½ cup milk
4-ounces mushrooms, finely diced
1 teaspoon butter
1 teaspoon kosher salt
½ teaspoon freshly cracked black pepper

DIRECTIONS

In a large skillet over medium heat, melt 1 teaspoon butter. Add mushrooms, salt and pepper, and sauté for about 7 minutes.

Add remaining butter and sprinkle with flour. Stir to combine and slowly whisk in broth and milk. Bring to a boil, reduce to a simmer, and simmer until thickened.

Garam Masala

INGREDIENTS

4 tablespoons black cumin seeds
2 bay leaves, crumbled
2 tablespoons green cardamom seeds
1 ½ teaspoons whole cloves
1 tablespoon fennel seeds
1 teaspoon fresh mace, chopped
1/8 teaspoon fresh nutmeg

DIRECTIONS

Heat a large skillet over medium heat. Add all ingredients except nutmeg and toast, about 8-10 minutes, until dry and fragrant. Remove from heat and add nutmeg. Transfer to spice grinder and pulse, until ground to a fine powder.

Fines Herbs

INGREDIENTS

2 tablespoons fresh Italian parsley, chopped

2 tablespoons fresh chervil, chopped

1 tablespoon fresh thyme, finely chopped

2 tablespoon fresh chives, minced

4 teaspoons fresh tarragon, minced

DIRECTIONS

Combine all ingredients. Use immediately.

About the

Author

After a couple of years of using Face Book as a pseudo food blog, I finally had several people tell me to just go ahead and jump in for real. I was a wienie for a while, (not knowing how to start) but jumped in over my head this past weekend. I decided to teach people how to cook like I do.

I love food. I grew up with a Mama and Granny who could cook, and my Daddy just LOVED food. That combination meant I sat on the kitchen counters when I was three, sticking my hands into everything I could and asking questions, and simultaneously was introduced to some very fine food in restaurants across the country and in Europe. In a nutshell, I was lucky.

I don't know why I was bitten. But I was - early and hard. I remember trying to write recipes when I couldn't have been older than 7. I actually still make the first 'real' recipe I ever created - something the family calls Potato Pancakes, and which is a combination of hash browns and traditional potato cakes.

I never went to culinary school. For some reason, it simply never occurred to me to pursue a professional career as a chef. I have however, been a student of technique for years and years now - how many is none of your business. But for a while. I love all food and classic cuisines - and I often go through phases, working my way through a technique until I have it mastered. Southern, French, Japanese, Californian, Indian, Chinese - I adore it all.

The result is I began picking up the 'why' of food, instead of just a collection of recipes. A few years ago I realized I no longer had to open a book to cook something, that I could taste a new food and analyze ingredients and cooking methods pretty accurately, and that I had a wealth of information rattling around in my head. My background is Southern, so of course that's a specialty. But to limit myself! The horror of never having a to-die-for pot au feu, or pot stickers, or tikka masala?...

BUT.

I have a tight budget. I have eight children of my own and four to six more that are huge presences in my life at any one moment. I have two dogs, including a baby ten-week old puppy. I have brothers and a sister, their children, my parents, and an INCREDIBLE group of friends and neighbors. I'm extremely busy to say the least. And because the children might want to build a tepee (right Tara?), or a snow fort, or forget to put on pants before they go outside, I can't normally tackle anything that has to be babysat on the stove or watch an oven carefully. I have to do things that are relatively easy AND on top of that - with ingredients and tools available in a tiny town in upper East Tennessee. That means real-world ingredients and no gourmet markets or supply stores.

So - I'm starting with some basics that several people have asked about. You'll see me do a lot of double duty meals - getting leftovers on purpose - but they'll never appear leftover. I'll show a lot of my favorite tricks and techniques - and of course I'll provide the recipes. The first couple are going to be a perfect brine and roast chicken. Simple - but with the clues to why the simple things are often the more difficult ones.

It took me a while to come up with a one sentence summary of how I cook. It came from a nickname a friend and neighbor gave me one night when I had "Frenched" some Southern-style green beans. French-delicious and Hillbilly became the Thrillbilly Gourmet. Classic technique to everyday food - but that's what it is. Most people have a dog underfoot and kids in and out of the kitchen while they cook. Or their sibs, spouses or parents. Friends and neighbors - and you'll meet all mine. Life is about distractions - and I wouldn't trade mine for anything. I cook good food. And I hope to teach you a little of what I know.

50052996R00135

Made in the USA
San Bernardino, CA
12 June 2017